This is a limited edition copy of the book Unashamed

Number 0878 of 1000

What others are saying about
Unashamed: Taking a Radical Stand for Christ

That must of been adrenalin I felt as I read Robby Gallaty's *Unashamed*. I sat up straighter in my chair, I was ready to sign up in the quest to make disciples. Unashamed is very important for a couple of reasons, it is passionate in its call to the life of following Christ. It also is built on solid exegesis, truths are most powerful when they flow out of the context of the biblical text. I know this, Robby Gallaty is on the move, he is leading and the question is, "Will you follow?"

Bill Hull, Author: *The Disciple Making Pastor, Christlike,* **and** *The Disciple Making Church*

In *Unashamed,* Robby Gallaty faithfully walks through the truths of God's Word in 2 Timothy. He uses both pointed exposition and personal experience to challenge readers to consider the risk and reward of following the call of Christ. I wholeheartedly recommend this pastor and this book to you.

Dr. David Platt, *New York Times* **Bestselling Author:** *Radical* **and Senior Pastor, The Church at Brook Hills, Birmingham, AL**

Unashamed is written by a "Young Timothy," Pastor Robby Gallaty, who pours his heart and mind into the study of Paul's second letter Timothy. With careful exegesis and warm pastoral application, Gallaty challenges both younger and older Christians alike to pursue a life of unashamed obedience to Jesus. In a day when many are interested in fads and famous rock-star church leaders, it is good to see a book emphasizing the heart of a disciple; namely, faithfulness to the Lord Jesus Christ. May this work be used to shape more young Timothy's into the image of Christ.

Dr. Tony Merida is the Teaching Pastor at Temple Baptist Church, MS

Robby Gallaty's *Unashamed* provides a powerful description of Paul's final instructions to Timothy on how to be a disciple (a learner, apprentice, or follower of Jesus), and how to make other disciples that is relevant to all Christians today. Filled with encouragement, practical illustrations, insightful analysis, and thoroughly biblical, I highly recommend this book for those who hunger for a deeper understanding of God's Word.

**Dr. John Ankerberg, Founder and President of
The Ankerberg Theological Research Institute, Chattanooga, TN**

This exposition of 2 Timothy combines careful attention to the text with practical applications. Reading it makes you realize that both the Apostle Paul and Robby Gallaty live in the real world with both the joys and disappointments of ministry. In these pages we are motivated to make those tough decisions needed for a life that honors the Lord without apology and without compromise.

Dr. Erwin Lutzer, The Moody Church, Chicago, IL

What a joy to witness the way the Lord has been using my friend, Robby Gallaty. Robby is a gifted pastor, strong leader, wonderful missionary statesman as well as a prolific writer. In *Unashamed: Taking A Radical Stand For Christ,* Robby masterfully dissects and exegetes the book of 2 Timothy in great detail and with great precision. You will be encouraged and greatly challenged by this "must read" book.

**Dr. Johnny M. Hunt, Former Southern Baptist Convention
President & Sr. Pastor, FBC Woodstock, GA**

"It is my great joy to recommend *Unashamed: Taking a Radical Stand for Christ.* Robby Gallaty has done something amazing—He has captured the heartbeat of the aged apostle as he leaves a legacy of faithful ministry to his beloved son in the faith. The timeless truths Robby shares from 2 Timothy make *Unashamed* a "must read" for anyone wanting to multiply disciples.

**Tim LaFleur, Discipler and Campus Minister,
Nicholls BCM, Thibodaux, LA**

taking a radical stand for Christ

ROBBY GALLATY

Unashamed:
Taking a Radical Stand for Christ

Copyright © 2010 by Robby Gallaty
Published by AMG Exposition, an imprint of
AMG Publishers, Inc.
6815 Shallowford Rd.
Chattanooga, Tennessee 37421

ISBN 13: 978-0-89957-957-3
ISBN 10: 0-89957-957-4
First Printing—October 2010

Cover designed by Jared Callais, Chattanooga, TN

Interior design and typesetting by Kristin Goble at PerfecType, Nashville, TN

Edited and proofread by Dillon Burroughs, Deb Strubel, Julie Golden, and Rick Steele

Printed in Canada

15 14 13 12 11 10 –T– 7 6 5 4 3 2 1

This book is dedicated to the members of Brainerd Baptist Church. Your encouragement and support motivated me to heed the charge spoken by Paul to Timothy: "preach the word." You have motivated me to be "Unashamed" of the gospel of the Lord Jesus Christ.

Acknowledgments

This book is the compilation of a series of expositional messages that I preached at Brainerd Baptist Church throughout 2009. As with any series, there are many who have participated in the process, whether knowingly or not. First, I would like to express my gratitude to the members of the Brainerd Baptist Church who were attentive every Sunday as I exposed God's Word to them. Not only was I given the opportunity to preach to them every week, but they also shaped me into a better preacher. Dr. Jim Shaddix was my first pastor and seminary professor. He modeled expository preaching through the messages he preached at Edgewater Baptist Church as well as the lectures he gave in *Proclaiming the Bible* class at the New Orleans Baptist Theological Seminary. The book he co-authored with Dr. Jerry Vines, *Power in the Pulpit,* has been a rich resource even till this day.

The assistance of John Fallahee was a crucial part of the sermon prep process. Over lunch every week, we outlined the passage from the Greek, recognized the central idea of the text, identified the theological theme, and sought to apply God's word in a relevant manner. I want to also thank Tim Lafleur, who was a sounding board for difficult passages that I came across. His influence many years ago on the importance of expository preaching laid a foundation for handling the Scriptures. Also,

Dillon Burroughs assisted in the initial process by submitting editorial advice. A special thanks to Julie Golden who proofread the final manuscript and offered needed revisions. Finally, thanks to my beautiful bride Kandi. Her constant support and understanding has allowed me to labor many late nights studying the Word. On many occasions, she has provided much needed insight, which I have used in my messages.

Foreword by Dr. Jerry Vines

The desire of Bible expositors of every generation is that there will be young preachers in the next generation who will continue the sacred craft. This was probably something of what Paul had in mind when he said to his young protégé, Timothy, "And the same things that thou hast heard of me among many witnesses, the same commit thou to faithful men, who shall be able to teach others also" (2 Timothy 2:2).

After preaching through books of the Bible for half a century, I am blessed to see a generation of young preachers who have determined to "preach the Word." That is why my heart has been blessed and my spirit refreshed to read this book of expository messages on 2 Timothy by Pastor Robby Gallaty. This young preacher, still fresh from a remarkable conversion experience, is giving himself to preaching through books of the Bible, book by book. No wonder his church is growing. No wonder his people at Brainerd Baptist Church in Chattanooga leave the services spiritually fed and satisfied.

Pastor Robby takes us through 2 Timothy paragraph by paragraph. In 16 chapters he causes this message of Paul to Timothy to come alive to God's people today. He makes the passage clear, giving appropriate background information, meanings of words, and clear exegesis of Scripture. Then, he makes the biblical text come alive with illustrations, many of them from his own life, and applies them winsomely to the lives of his hearers.

This is soon-to-be "Dr. Gallaty's" second book. It will not be the last. I predict many more will come from his keen mind, fervent heart and dedicated will. And, I pray many other young pastors will follow the example of Robby Gallaty.

Dr. Jerry Vines
former pastor, First Baptist Church, Jacksonville, FL

Table of Contents

Introduction

My spiritual life has been profoundly impacted by men who were mature in their walk with Christ and were willing to train me according to the apostle Paul's model for discipleship. We find this model in the book of 2 Timothy, written by Paul while he was held in chains in Rome. His life was in danger, and he desperately needed support and comfort from his fellow believers, but almost all had turned away. Paul's relationship with Timothy was such that he sent for Timothy to come to Rome and be with him. Yet many scholars believe the letter indicates Paul feared his death would come before Timothy arrived. The message Paul chose to pass on to Timothy in what he feared could be their last communication is one that echoes my heart's desire. Paul's exhortation to Timothy to carry on in discipleship mirrors the lessons I have learned through my own struggles as a new believer.

There was a time in my life when the Lord was very distant from me. I was raised in a very strict Roman Catholic family and attended a Catholic parochial school for boys. In my mind, participation in religion included attending Mass on Sundays, checking a mental box for attendance. Each Sunday I came to church governed by a personal philosophy to do what was best for myself, with no regard for God. I left the services with an unchanged heart.

After high school, I was awarded a basketball scholarship at the University of North Carolina Greensboro. It was an amazing opportunity that was thwarted when my girlfriend at the time begged me to reconsider and attend a college closer to home. I opened a phone book to look at colleges closer to home, and came across William Carey University. Although the players for the team had already been picked, I begged the coach for a chance to try out. The very next day the coach called to tell me that I had made the team and would be receiving a scholarship to play for William Carrey.

Two weeks after I started school, my girlfriend who had convinced me to give up playing for UNC Greensboro, broke up with me. I didn't know it at the time, but God was working in my life to prepare me for something great. During my second semester at William Carey, a friend named Jeremy Brown approached me to discuss what it really meant to have a relationship with God and surrender my life to Him. Although I refused to hear his words at that time, his persistent message that God would forgive anything I had done in the past or in the future if I would only cry out to Him remained in my heart. Years later those words would come back to me at the time I needed them the most.

After graduating from college, I started a computer business with two friends. We spent six months putting everything we could into the company, but things never took off. Our company was dismantled, and we each parted our separate ways. I was drawn to No Holds Barred fighting competitions and began to train in Brazilian Jiu-Jitsu. I was six foot six and 295 pounds. I worked as a bouncer at a club in New Orleans during Mardi Gras, where I was paid to fight. It was exhilarating, but also dangerous. I felt I was indestructible.

All of those feelings ended on November 22, 1999, when an 18-wheeler swerved across two lanes of traffic and rear-ended me at 65 miles per hour, slamming my car into a guardrail. The doctors determined I had two herniated discs in my neck, one herniated disc in my back, and one bulging disc in my lower back. The doctors sent me home with prescriptions for Oxycontin, Valium, Soma, and Percocet. Never having taken drugs before, I began by taking the medications according to prescription. Within three months I was addicted to pharmaceutical drugs. When I realized my thirty-day supply was running low as a result of over-consumption, I turned to other means of feeding my insatiable need to get high.

It was at this point that two acquaintances introduced me to the potentially lucrative business possibilities in the drug arena. I was quickly able to use my knowledge of the business world and the skills I had gained through owning my own computer company to begin a business importing and dealing illegal drugs. With the help of a few others, I trafficked illegal drugs such as heroin, cocaine, GHB, marijuana, and various pharmaceuticals into the city of New Orleans. We felt like we had it all. By the world's standard, it was the life that many only dream about.

But in 2000, it all started to spiral out of control with the death of a close friend. Rick died from a heroin overdose with the needle still in his arm. Between 2000 and 2003 I lost eight friends to alcohol or drug-related deaths. Six other friends ended up in prison. Our operation was being investigated, with the police interested in our particular group. Suddenly we couldn't pay the bills. The gas, water, and electricity to our house were shut off. The bill collectors continued to call until the phone was turned off as well. At this point it was costing $160 a day to feed my addiction.

When I realized I had reached the end of my rope, I begged my parents for a second chance. Given what I had done to them months before, I didn't expect their sympathy or assistance. I had robbed my father of $15,000 in those months by using his credit card information to buy items online that I could later pawn or sell for drug money. When my parents learned what I had done, they were devastated and furious. They had warned me not to return to their house, but God's mercy was present the day I begged for forgiveness and pleaded for help on their living room floor. I didn't expect or deserve a second chance from my parents, but they gave me one and took me in.

My next step was a rehab program in Tijuana, Mexico, of all places. I spent ten days going through an intensive recovery program involving the injection of amino acids to realign the serotonin and dopamine levels in my body. When I completed the program, I moved to Mobile, Alabama, to be with my sister. Things began to improve. I got a job as a sales manager at Powerhouse Gym, where I began to train five days a week. In what I now can assure you was a terribly bad idea, I attempted to squat over 500 pounds.

I saw the doctor in New Orleans, where I learned that I had damaged the same disc in my back, which would require immediate surgery. Following the surgery, I was sent home with another full prescription for the same pain meds I was prescribed after my car accident. For the next six months I allowed these medications that had caused so much hurt and heartache back into my family, where things quickly fell to pieces. Knowing I had reached rock bottom, I detoxed myself and voluntarily re-entered rehab.

On my first night there, November 12, 2002, I remembered the words spoken to me by Jeremy Brown, who had told me that no matter what you've done, Christ wants to love you and is waiting for you to call out to him. It didn't happen in a church service, under a revival tent, or on a crusade. Jesus chose to meet me right in my room. As I surrendered that night, I made a decision to ask God to save me from the mess I had created. I repented of my sinful lifestyle and experienced God's forgiveness. I also made two additional promises. The first is that I would completely devote 100 percent of my life to Him. The second is that I would travel the world sharing the story of what God had done in my life.

I spent the next twenty-four hours in that room with the Lord Jesus Christ. The experience moved me to the point that I couldn't hold back my excitement. That day I told my dad that I intended to become a preacher. My father was confused and concerned about how my plans for marriage would work. Since he raised me in a devoutly Catholic home, he assumed I wanted to become a priest.

I explained that I was ready to leave behind my focus on ritual and performance and become a preacher who focused on bringing people into a relationship with God. However, it was difficult to make this transition. I came from a church that didn't promote Scripture reading and memorization or extemporaneous prayer. For several months, I wandered aimlessly in my Christian life, uncertain of how to proceed and growing stagnant. It was then that a church member suggested that I pray for God to provide me with a mentor to disciple me the way Paul discipled Timothy. It was something I was unfamiliar with and unsure of, but I began to pray.

Only a few weeks later, another church member named David Platt approached me about meeting once a week for Bible study, Scripture memorization, and prayer. He asked that I pray about whether or not this was the right decision, but I was able to tell him I had already been in prayer. God had heard my cry and had started working in David's heart to provide me with a mentor before I even knew I needed one. For the next five months, I met with David weekly to discuss the glory of God, the lost nature of man, and the good news of Christ. It was during this time that David encouraged and strengthened my desire to share my story and begin to reach others, using discipleship and expository preaching.

That summer, I was offered a chance to work with Tim LaFleur as a campus pastor for Highpoint in Glorieta, New Mexico. Tim's ministry at Nicholls State University has given him the opportunity to disciple hundreds of college students into mature followers of Christ. We spent that summer discussing the doctrines of the Christian life, the empowerment of the Holy Spirit, the equipping of saints, and assurance of salvation.

These men were the Pauls in my life, who opened their arms, took me in, and taught me what it means to be a Christian. But, like Paul, they didn't just teach me how to live a Spirit-filled life. These men didn't stop at making a difference in my own life, they instructed, demonstrated, and challenged me to do the same for others. Paul's instructions to Timothy were to continue to replicate what he learned from him. Prayerfully, you will be challenged through this book and through the Word of God to do the same.

chapter one

Following the Call of Christ

2 TIMOTHY 1:1-2

The Bible tells us a lot about the life of Paul, but many of us don't know more than the basic details. A closer look at his final letter can give us insight into Paul's life and experiences, as well as an understanding of the powerful words and instructions left by this hero of the faith. In the book of 2 Timothy, we find Paul's last letter to the son of his heart, beginning with the powerful, though brief, words introducing us to the message Paul desperately needed to convey:

> 1 Paul, an apostle of Christ Jesus by the will of God according to the promise of the life that is in Christ Jesus,
> 2 To Timothy, my beloved child:
> Grace, mercy, and peace from God the Father and Christ Jesus our Lord.

How easy it is to skim past an introduction. I'm often tempted to skip the author's opening notes on background and influences and go straight for the meat of the story. But it would be a mistake to quickly dismiss these verses as the mere opening of a letter, with no more significance than we would give to writing "Dear Friend" as we open an email. We must remember that every word of the Bible is divinely inspired and useful for teaching. Each word can impart wisdom and insight.

To begin this letter, Paul reveals to us that he considered Timothy "my beloved child." From the opening of the letter we are not only learning about the characters of Paul and Timothy, but also about their special relationship forged through discipleship. When Paul first met Timothy, he realized Timothy had a mother who was a devout Jew and faithful to God. Likewise, Timothy's grandmother was also Jewish and a devout worshiper of God. But his father was Greek, likely following the gods of Greco-Roman culture rather than Christ.

Fortunately, Timothy didn't follow in the footsteps of his father. How do we know? 2 Timothy 1:5 notes, "I am reminded of your sincere faith, a faith that dwelt first in your grandmother Lois and your mother Eunice and now, I am sure, dwells in you as well." Timothy's spiritual heritage resulted from the leadership of the women in his family.

When Paul met him in Acts 16, Timothy was probably fifteen or sixteen years old. About fifteen years later, Paul wrote these words to Timothy: "Let no one despise you for your youth, but set the believers an example in speech, in conduct, in love, in faith, in purity" (1 Timothy 4:12). We often use this verse to inspire our teenagers or even our younger children. But it's likely that Timothy was thirty when Paul wrote these words to him.

Historically, we are not certain how involved Timothy was in Paul's missionary journeys. We do know, however, that he accompanied Paul and Silas on a number of journeys at a young age. Isn't it encouraging to know that Paul entrusted the gospel of the Lord Jesus Christ to a young man? It's heartening for us to realize that even if we think "God can't use me because I'm young," God can use us in a mighty way, just like He did with Timothy regardless of age.

But this passage doesn't just teach us about Timothy. In the first verse, Paul introduces himself to us as "an apostle of Christ Jesus by the will of God. . . ." We tend to focus on the character of Timothy and his call to serve God despite his youth, but in these verses, we learn equally about Paul's call to serve Christ. Understanding Paul's history as a Christian is vital to understanding his role as discipler of Timothy, his charge to Timothy to carry on the work of discipleship, and our role as Christians to be imitators of the Word. In the remainder of this chapter, we'll discover three key progressions in his life that provide deep and meaningful applications for our lives today.

Prior to the Call

Paul was not always a Christian. In fact, before Jesus Christ called him, Paul's life was radically different. In Philippians 3:4–5, Paul shares, "If anyone else thinks he has reason for confidence in the flesh, I have more: circumcised on the eighth day, of the people of Israel, of the tribe of Benjamin, a Hebrew of Hebrews." Prior to his calling to follow Christ, Paul's focus is first on the importance of his *ancestry*. Jewish scripture and tradition teaches that the Hebrew nation is chosen by God. Acceptance and spiritual significance to the Jews of the time began with ethnicity. Without the family background, Paul would have been just another Gentile. However, his ability to identify not only with the Hebrew people, but with the tribe of Benjamin, won him acceptance in the Jewish community.

Paul also focuses on his *achievements*. He notes, "As to righteousness under the law, blameless." Other translations use the word "perfect." Paul is communicating, "When you looked at me, you noticed I was a Pharisee." Acts 23:6 informs us that Paul's own father was a Pharisee. Paul had a strong lineage. Not only could he identify with the Jewish people with regards to his ethnicity and heritage, but his own life was a paragon of Jewish virtue. He was educated in the Law and fervent in his obedience.

Look at how Paul proves his point. In Philippians 3:6, he writes, "As to zeal, a persecutor of the church." He says in essence, "Not only did I tell people about God, I violently and aggressively persecuted those who followed Jesus, the one Jews considered a false Messiah." The newly formed Christian movement included Jews who claimed, "Jesus is God." In the Jewish tradition, if someone called anyone other than Yahweh God, they were criminals. They were breaking the Law. Why? They were blaspheming the name of the Lord. Paul added to his impressive resume the fact that he had persecuted anyone who said Jesus was Lord. If you had looked at Paul by his culture's standards and by the Jewish church's standards, you would have been impressed. He seemed to have it all together.

The twist to this passage comes with the use of the word "but" in verse 7. This small word points out a remarkable contrast that altered the course of Paul's life. When Paul writes, "*But* whatever gain I had, I counted as loss for the sake of Christ," he says in essence, "Everything in my past amounts to nothing compared to the surpassing value of knowing Christ Jesus my Lord."

The comparison between Paul's external qualifications and the "surpassing greatness" of knowing Christ highlights the first step in the progression. Paul thought he had it all, but once he recognized the love Christ offers, he considered his life prior to the call as nothing in comparison. Nothing he had earned through lineage, education, or achievements could compare to the experience of Christ.

The Call

Paul's salvation experience can be found in Acts 9. It is in this chapter that we see God intervene dramatically in the life of Paul (known as Saul at the time). Verses 1–9 read:

1 But Saul, still breathing threats and murder against the disciples of the Lord, went to the high priest 2 and asked him for letters to the synagogues at Damascus, so that if he found any belonging to the Way, men or women, he might bring them bound to Jerusalem. 3 Now as he went on his way, he approached Damascus, and suddenly a light from heaven flashed around him. 4 And falling to the ground he heard a voice saying to him, "Saul, Saul, why are you persecuting me?" 5 And he said, "Who are you, Lord?" And he said, "I am Jesus, whom you are persecuting. 6 But rise and enter the city, and you will be told what you are to do." 7 The men who were traveling with him stood speechless, hearing the voice but seeing no one.

This is the second act in Paul's redemption story. He was traveling along the road to Damascus to arrest Christians, bring them back to Jerusalem, and place them on trial for preaching that Jesus is Lord. Along the way to Damascus, Paul saw a light, he heard a voice, and he obeyed. Jesus spoke to Paul in an unexpected but unmistakable voice, revealing himself as Yahweh. Following the vision, Paul found himself temporarily blinded. Three days later, a man by the name of Ananias who lived in Damascus was commanded by God to find and instruct Paul. Look at God's words in verses 15–16: But the Lord said to him, "Go, for he is a chosen instrument of mine to carry my name before the Gentiles and kings and the children of Israel. For I will show him how much he must suffer for the sake of my name."

Before Paul ever began his ministry, Ananias revealed to him that he would suffer greatly for the cause he had only days before been instrumental in persecuting. Can you imagine Paul saying, "Mom and Dad, guess what? God has called me to serve the Lord Jesus. And guess what the best thing is? I get to suffer throughout the process." Not too exciting, right? In a matter of days, Paul not only gave up his heritage, his place of privilege in the Jewish community, and everything he had worked for his entire life, but also learned that doing so would mean great suffering. Is it any wonder that some of us suffer? The greatest apostle, the super apostle of the Lord Jesus Christ was told, "You'll face hardship, there are going to be insults against you, there will be turmoil and torture. But keep going, don't fall back." That was the call of the apostle Paul.

After the Call

Following his call, Paul continued to obey the instructions given to him by his Lord and disappeared into Arabia. Galatians 1 offers the background to this time period.

> 14 And I was advancing in Judaism beyond many of my own age among my people, so extremely zealous was I for the traditions of my fathers. 15 But when he who had set me apart before I was born, and who called me by his grace, 16 was pleased to reveal his Son to me, in order that I might preach him among the Gentiles, I did not immediately consult with anyone; 17 nor did I go up to Jerusalem to those who were apostles before me, but I went away into Arabia, and returned again to Damascus.

How long did Paul stay in Arabia? Three *years*. The number three should tell you something. This is the same amount of time that Jesus spent on earth with His disciples. He called them to follow Him and for three straight years He ministered to them, taught them, and trained them. In this passage, we see that Paul's life parallels the lives of Christ's disciples. Paul even stated at one point in the Bible that he was "untimely born," feeling as if he should have been born at the time of Christ and been among His disciples (see 1 Corinthians 15:8). Yet, like the Twelve, Jesus trained and prepared Paul for three long years before Paul's missionary journeys began.

When Paul returned to the scene three years later, Galatians 1:23–24 notes the response of the Christian believers: "They only were hearing it said, 'He who used to persecute us is now preaching the faith he once tried to destroy.' And they glorified God because of me." Now imagine a person who had been arresting and persecuting Christians in this country suddenly telling people to follow Jesus. Many of us are skeptical when a public figure who has lived a lifestyle glorifying the rejection of Christ suddenly announces a public conversion. The believers in Paul's culture were cynical as well. But would we praise God if we discovered this person to be true to his word? Definitely.

Paul's First Missionary Journey (app. 46–47 A.D.)

After three years of preparations with Christ, Paul began the first of his major missionary journeys. These are found in Acts chapters 13–15 and took place from approximately 46 to 47 A.D., only about fifteen years after the resurrection of Jesus. Paul started the first missionary journey by traveling through Cyprus and Asia Minor (modern-day Turkey), launching churches, and preaching the gospel. His first letter during this trip was to the Galatians, explaining his past lifestyle and the extraordinary transformation to some of his early Gentile converts.

Paul's Second Missionary Journey (app. 49–51 A.D.)

After returning to his sending church of Antioch, Paul soon regrouped and headed out again on his second missionary journey from approximately 49 to 51 A.D., contained in chapters 16–18 in Acts. Acts 16:1–2 begins this sequence, stating, "Paul came also to Derbe and to Lystra. A disciple was there, named Timothy, the son of a Jewish woman who was a believer, but his father was a Greek. He was well spoken of by the brothers at Lystra and Iconium."

This church, located in Ephesus, would receive more letters from Paul than any other. The book of Ephesians is named for the first letter Paul sent. First and 2 Timothy were also written to believers in Ephesus. Even Acts has a special section focused on Ephesus. Finally, the book of Revelation also includes a brief letter to the church at Ephesus in its letters to the seven churches.

Why did Paul place such an importance on the Ephesian believers? One reason is because that was where Timothy was leading the church. It's vitally important for us to know about the context of the church in Ephesus as we study the life of Paul speaking to his protégé Timothy. Paul left Philippi and began to travel throughout the region. From Philippi he moved to Athens, then Galatia, and then Thessalonica in modern-day Greece. Paul also included stops at Corinth and Ephesus during his second missionary journey. During this time Paul wrote 1 and 2 Thessalonians before returning once again to his home base in Antioch.

Paul's Third Missionary Journey (56–57 A.D.)

Within a year or less of his return from the second journey, Paul embarked on his third and longest missionary journey from approximately 52 to 57 A.D., found in chapters 18–20 in Acts. Once again, in Acts 18:24, we find Paul in Ephesus, the city where Timothy is in leadership at the time Paul wrote 2 Timothy.

During these years, Paul also wrote his longest letters. These include 1 and 2 Corinthians and the letter to the believers in Rome in approximately 57 A.D. Finally, at the end of Acts 20, we find Paul meeting one last time with the leaders of the Ephesian church before departing for Jerusalem, a place where he anticipates increased persecution.

Paul's Caesarean Imprisonment (app. 58–59 A.D.)

Because of the controversy caused by Paul's conversion, some of the leading Jews in Jerusalem planned to arrest him. The arrest was originally made because of an accusation that Paul had taken a Gentile (non-Jew) into the Jewish Temple, causing an uproar among the local Jews. Everywhere Paul traveled, people persecuted him for the sake of the gospel. His life reveals a striking application for our lives. As contemporary Christians in Western society, we live in a country where religious liberty is assumed. But we fail to recognize there are brothers and sisters in Christ right now all over the world who are dependent upon the

Holy Spirit for safety every single day. In one-fourth of the world's countries, fifty-one nations, there is some kind of official condemnation against openly sharing Christ.

Friends, the apostle Paul experienced the horrors of persecution on a regular basis. When Paul was thrown into prison while visiting Jerusalem, he had to endure the laborious Roman judicial system. Following his arrest, Paul spent two years in Caesarea while it was under the leadership of Governor Felix. Felix kept him in prison for those two years because he thought Paul would attempt to bribe him.

Judicial corruption was common during the first-century Roman occupation of Israel. Prisoners would offer a financial bribe or other incentive to a leader, and the leader would in return free them from prison. Paul chose not to compromise with the corrupt political system of his time. As a result, he remained in prison for two years until Felix lost his office to Festus. Festus sent Paul to Jerusalem for a hearing where Paul invoked his right as a Roman citizen to be tried before Caesar.

Around 60 A.D., Paul was shipped by boat to Rome based on his appeal to Festus. On the voyage to Rome, the ship was destroyed in a terrible storm. Paul was thrown overboard with the rest of the prisoners, who were forced either to swim or grab parts of the boat to survive. Those who survived, including Paul, were able to find refuge on the island of Malta. Paul remained under guard there for three months. Finally, he boarded a second ship under Roman guard and headed toward Rome. Upon arriving at the nearest port to the Roman capital, Paul headed straight to jail again, spending the next two years under house arrest. According to scholarly estimates, Paul spent 25 percent of his missionary time incarcerated.

Paul's First Roman Imprisonment (app. 60–62 A.D.)

In J. W. McGarvey's commentary on the life of Paul, he stated, "No two years of Paul's life were better filled with earnest labor than the two years he spent in Rome under house arrest."[1] The fact that Paul was under house arrest at this point is significant. There were two types of prison sentences in Rome. The first and preferred choice was house arrest or house prison. The last chapter of Acts ends with Paul in this Roman house prison.

These two years are considered some of Paul's most influential because it was during this two-year period that he wrote several of our New Testament letters. These include Philemon, Philippians, Ephesians, and Colossians. When you realize the circumstances under which these letters were written, you'll never read these letters the same way again. It's easy for someone to quote from Philippians, "Rejoice in the Lord always, and again I say rejoice" when they are having a good day. But Paul was a prisoner at the moment he penned these words, and had been for an extended period of time.

If you had enough money in Rome, the government often allowed prisoners to rent a home. Paul probably stayed on the third floor of his rented quarters because the first floor would have been reserved for shops and the second floor would have been more expensive than the third floor. In addition, he probably had people bringing him food.

We don't know all the details, but we know that Paul was forced to pay for his way through prison. As he was under house arrest, Paul dictated and penned letters for His Lord Jesus Christ. In Philippians 1, we hear of some of Paul's guards turning to Christ. Paul even shared in Acts 28 that the Roman authorities let people visit him. The final verse of Acts well summarizes, "He lived there two whole years at his own expense, and welcomed all who came to him, proclaiming the kingdom of God and teaching about the Lord Jesus Christ with all boldness and without hindrance."

Paul's Second Roman Imprisonment (app. 64–65 A.D.)

Paul's life and the life of Christians during this period were radically changed by the events surrounding the emperor of the time—Nero

Claudius Caesar. The events I believe led to Paul's final imprisonment occurred under this man's reign.

Nero was the Emperor of Rome from AD 54 to 67 and was known as a vicious man. Many speculate that the modern day diagnosis of bipolar disorder could be applied to Nero. The buffer provided by Cynecca and Buras, his trusted advisors, allowed his first five years of rule to pass without any significant incident. But Nero's mental state continued to deteriorate, and he became increasingly paranoid and power hungry. He eventually killed every single person standing in the way of his control, including his own mother.

In AD 64 Nero wanted to make room for more buildings in Rome and set a small fire on one of the houses. The fire raged out of control and burned down half of Rome. Seeking a scapegoat, Nero blamed the growing number of Roman Christians. Historically, we are told that Paul was arrested during the persecution against Roman Christians at this time, as he had returned to the city once again as a missionary.

Acts chapter 28 ends with Paul living in a house prison. After this period of house arrest, Paul was imprisoned in Rome in the Mamertine prison, the Roman equivalent of a maximum-security jail. This was vastly different from Paul's house prison experience. Look at what commentator John McCray says of the apostle Paul's experience in approximately AD 65 as he waited for trial in Mamertine:

> Roman imprisonment was preceded by being stripped naked and then flogged. A humiliating, painful, and bloody ordeal. The bleeding wounds went untreated as prisoners sat in painful leg and wrist chains. Mutilated, blood-stained clothes were not replaced even in the cold of winter. . . . Most cells were dark, especially the inner cell of the prison like the one Paul was in. Unbearable cold, lack of water, cramped quarters, and sickening stench from the few toilets made sleeping difficult and waking hours miserable. Because of the miserable conditions many prisoners begged for a speedy death. Many committed suicide in their own cells because they couldn't take it anymore. Paul was eventually rearrested and

brought this time not to a house prison in Rome, but brought to a prison. A prison that was evidently difficult to find.[2]

In 2 Timothy 1:16–18 we are told, "May the Lord grant mercy to the household of Onesiphorus, for he often refreshed me and was not ashamed of my chains, but when he arrived in Rome he searched for me earnestly and found me—may the Lord grant him to find mercy from the Lord on that Day!"

Paul was probably so secluded from everyone that his friends could not find him. He would likely have been lowered down into a dungeon-like cave and left with little food or water and only a small hole to allow oxygen and light. That's how the apostle Paul lived out the final days or possibly months of his life before he was beheaded and killed for the sake of the gospel.

Paul wrote the letter we know as 2 Timothy while confined to this dungeon-like cell. He wrote to Timothy describing the freezing cold and his desire for a blanket and his books. He told Timonty he was about to be poured out as a drink offering, a clear metaphor referring to his pending death. Evidently he had already been summoned to trial once and knew death was imminent. With this background, we reflect on the opening words of Paul to his son in the faith, Timothy. With his earthly life nearing a dark end, Paul reached out one last time, saying, "Timothy, listen, this is my final love letter to you. Listen to its words. Keep the faith. Follow the call." These words were recorded not only for Timothy, but for those of us who long to live out an extreme faith in following Christ today.

One Final Letter

Imagine that before your father died, he took the time to write you a note. He told you about problems to avoid in life. He guided you in the right direction for the future. He encouraged you. He gave you instructions on how to live the rest of your life. If you were like me, you would cherish that note because it was the last letter your father wrote to you.

Paul, as a spiritual father to his spiritual son, Timothy, wrote such a letter to him just before his death, and opened with these words: "Paul, an apostle of Christ Jesus, by the will of God, according to the promise of the life in Christ Jesus." He wrote this clearly knowing that he would soon be executed. He knew men could destroy the body, but that we can have eternal life in Christ Jesus. Why? Because Jesus Christ is the only one who rose from the dead and lives for eternity. In my mind, Paul was saying something like this: "Timothy, don't worry about me. Don't worry about what I'm in, because I am here by the will of God. According to the promise of the life of Christ Jesus grace, mercy, and peace be with you. And Timothy—here it is—here's my last will and testament for you."

I challenge you to reflect upon the pages of this book as we study Paul's final words in his earthly life. Together, we will experience a greater understanding of God's call for our lives, His will for our lives, and how His promises can change us and others, now and for eternity.

chapter 2

Living with Courageous Faith

Take a moment to think back over the centuries and try to imagine the weight and importance of this letter that Timothy received from Paul. I like to picture young Timothy pondering these profound words of encouragement that he received from his spiritual father and mentor in the faith. Here's what Paul writes, beginning with verse 3:

> 3 I thank God whom I serve, as did my ancestors, with a clear conscience, as I remember you constantly in my prayers night and day. 4 As I remember your tears, I long to see you, that I may be filled with joy. 5 I am reminded of your sincere faith, a faith that dwelt first in your grandmother Lois and your mother Eunice and now, I am sure, dwells in you as well. 6 For this reason, I remind you to fan into flame the gift of God, which is in you through the laying on of my hands, 7 for God gave us a spirit not of fear but of power and love and self-control.

Remember the Past

In this inspiring passage, Paul calls Timothy to be bold and courageous in his faith. The text contains two main themes. I consider the first section a passage of *remembrance*. Paul uses the terminology "I remember" or "I am reminded" in each of the first three verses. In verse 3, *Paul remembers his own life*. He writes, "I thank God whom I serve, as did my ancestors, with a clear conscience, as I *remember* you." In verse 4, Paul also says, "As I *remember*." And then in verse 5, he says, "I am *reminded* of your sincere faith."

Paul begins by saying, "I thank God . . . , as did my ancestors." This is an interesting twist because Paul is writing to Timothy, so you would think that Paul would start out by thanking Timothy, right? "Timothy, thank you for your investment in the kingdom of God. Thank you for your discipleship, your passion." But instead, Paul says, "I thank God whom I serve."

Remember that Paul is writing this letter from a filthy Roman prison where he has experienced physical and emotional devastation brought on by flogging, starvation, unbearable living conditions, and humiliation. It's easy to thank God when things are going well in your life. But how do you react when your circumstances take a turn for the worse? Paul is suffering in one of the most horrible places imaginable, yet he still has an attitude of appreciation to the Lord.

In essence, Paul says, "Timothy, I have no regrets. I thank God whom I serve. You know that I'm in prison. It's dark. It's cold. It's wet. It's filthy. I'm starving. But I have no animosity toward anyone. I'm not angry at the corrupt politicians who locked me up. I simply thank God whom I serve."

How about you? Do you take time to thank God even when your life circumstances are difficult or even devastating? Not only did Paul thank God, he continued to serve God, even from the confinement of prison. Paul may have been chained and alone, but he still served through *worship* and *prayer*. Often, we limit our definition of the term *worship* to singing songs of praise to the Lord. But it's so much more than that. Do you consider your every day activities, even those that are dull or monotonous to be an act of worship? I don't know about you, but just hearing a man who is truly suffering in prison under unimaginable conditions saying, "I thank God whom I serve" is enough to motivate me. Paul passionately urges Timothy to follow his example by continuing in confident service, regardless of how bleak the situation may appear.

Paul also emphasizes his continual prayer for Timothy. Paul is not exaggerating his devotion to prayer. I really believe he was praying for Timothy night and day. I have no doubt that he spent many hours kneeling in that filthy prison cell, engaging in intercessory prayer for Timothy as well as many others in the faith. Paul even told the Thessalonian church in 1 Thessalonians 5:17 to pray *without ceasing.*

I believe the apostle was at a place in his life where he enjoyed constant communion with God. I'm not talking about simply saying grace at mealtimes or repeating rote prayers over and over. Paul lived and breathed a life of prayer. He was bent on doing God's will and staying in perfect communion with the Lord. That type of communion involves not just talking to the Lord and asking Him for what we need, but also listening to what God has to say to us each day.

Paul not only remembers his own life, but also remembers Timothy's *life of service.* "As I remember your tears," Paul writes, "I long to see you, that I may be filled with joy." During Paul's second missionary journey, he extended the arm of fellowship to Timothy, inviting him to join the journey and take part in spreading the gospel to the nations. After that, Timothy often accompanied Paul in his ministry and is referred to in seven of Paul's letters: Romans, 2 Corinthians, Philippians, Colossians, 1 Thessalonians, 2 Thessalonians, and Philemon. Two of the letters reveal occasions on which Paul sent Timothy to minister in his place (1 and 2 Thessalonians). And, of course, Paul addressed two letters directly to Timothy (1 and 2 Timothy)

Paul considered Timothy to be the son he never had, his spiritual child in the faith. And Paul was tenderly saying, "Timothy, I remember your tears." We don't know exactly why Timothy had been crying. Some scholars believe that Timothy cried because Paul left him to continue to spread the gospel, and Timothy knew that these journeys would eventually lead Paul to prison and to death. Other commentators believe that Timothy wept tears of joy when he was ordained to the ministry by Paul. Regardless, we know that Timothy wept when Paul left. We also know that Timothy was not the only believer disheartened by Paul's departure. We read in Acts 20:26–38: "And when he had said these things, he (Paul) knelt down and prayed with them all. There was much weeping on the part of all; they embraced Paul and kissed him. Being sorrowful, most of all, because of the word he had spoken, that they would not see his face again. And they accompanied him to the ship."

Timothy's sorrow is understandable when we realize the depth of his relationship with Paul. Paul stepped into the life of Timothy to be his spiritual father. It seems clear that Timothy's father was not in the picture. Timothy's situation reminds me of just how difficult it is for believers in Jesus Christ whose fathers weren't there for them. If you who didn't have a dad who loved, cared for, and provided for you, it may be difficult for you to fully embrace God as your loving heavenly Father. You may have trouble believing that God could truly be gracious, loving, and forgiving.

Thankfully, God brought Paul into Timothy's life to take the spiritual place his father should have occupied. But, as a father figure, Paul knew that Timothy needed to leave the spiritual nest and begin discipling others. If you are a parent, you know that in order for your child to develop into a successful, mature adult, he or she must be required to take on increasing responsibility. At some point, however difficult for both parent and child, the child must move forward in independence and start a separate life. Paul knew that in order for Timothy to continue to mature in his faith and to become an independent follower of Christ, contributing to the growth of others, he would have to push Timothy to face these responsibilities on his own. Timothy may have protested that he wasn't ready or couldn't handle the burden of pastoring a church alone, but Paul knew that God had equipped Timothy for service.

And with tears filling his eyes, Timothy saw his spiritual father leave—Paul, the man who had stepped into his life to mentor, encourage, and comfort him.

Finally, *Paul remembers Timothy's lineage.* He assures Timothy that the faith of his grandmother, Lois, and his mother, Eunice, has been passed on to Timothy as well. What a great spiritual heritage was given to Timothy by his mother and grandmother. They invested deeply in the life of Timothy. Paul uses the word Greek word for *sincere* here. The word *sincere* in Greek is a negative prefix attached to the word *hupokritos*, which is where we get the English word *hypocrite*. By using this prefix, Paul is saying that Timothy's faith is not hypocritical. It is sincere; it is genuine.

This verse should greatly encourage mothers and grandmothers who are the only Christian influences in the lives of their offspring. These two women had an investment that we read about even to this day. They are even mentioned by name, which is somewhat rare in scripture.

In today's words, Paul says, "Listen, it wasn't just your grandmother and your mother, it was the Word of God that you knew from your childhood that was able to make you wise unto salvation through faith in Christ Jesus." The women in Timothy's life provided him with a strong, godly heritage. Through their influence combined with the power of God's Word, Timothy was brought to salvation.

Cultivate Your Gift

The second theme of this passage is a direct response to remembrances of the first theme. In light of the testimony Timothy is encouraged to remember from Paul's life, his own life, and his upbringing, he is commanded to respond by *cultivating his gift*. Paul might say it this way today: "Because of these things, you must do this: fan into flame the gift of God which was given to you through the laying on of my hands." The Greek term translated *fan into flame* means "to kindle afresh, to revive." In other words, this was a flame that was about to go out. Paul is telling Timothy, "Your spiritual fire was burning hot, but now the flame is barely flickering. Fan it back to life, Timothy. Be courageous in sharing the gospel."

This spiritual fire is the gift of God, both to Timothy and to us as believers in Christ. Aren't you glad that we have the gift of God? This gift is within us; nobody can steal it away. This verse reminds me of Psalm 119:11, where David says, "I have stored your word up in my heart, that I might not sin against you." Once you have memorized scripture, and you have stored it in your mind and heart, it lives within you—no one can take that from you. But it can lie dormant. If you're a believer in Jesus Christ, you have been given the gift from God. The question is, are you using His gift for God's glory, or are you letting it lie dormant?

The Greek word *charisma* is where we get the English word *charismatic*. This term describes the gift of God. And notice that Paul tells Timothy, it's a singular gift. You would think Paul might say, "Timothy, fan into the flame the gifts [plural] of God," but he doesn't. He says "the gift of God." The apostle Peter uses the same terminology in 1 Peter 4:10 when he writes to the church, "As each of you has received a gift [singular], use it to serve one another." Paul himself uses a similar idea in Galatians 5:22 to describe the fruit of the Holy Spirit. He doesn't say the "fruits" of the Spirit; he says, the "fruit" (singular) of the Spirit: love, joy, peace, patience, kindness, goodness, faithfulness, gentleness, and self-control.

When you came to Christ, you said, "God, I confess of my sins and I repent of anything I've done against You. I believe that Jesus is Lord, and I ask you to fill me with the Holy Spirit." When the Holy Spirit fills you by the power of God, you have all the giftedness you need in Christ. Did you know that? He's given you all the fruit that you need.

Unfortunately, some of us hinder the manifestation of the Spirit's gift in our life.

When you gave your life to the Lord, it is as if God credited your account, saying, "My account is your account. You have resources to use that are endless. You have the full bank account of heaven." The problem is, many of us aren't tapping into God's account and utilizing those resources. Hudson Taylor once said, "Depend on it, God's work, done in God's way, will never lack God's supplies."[3]

In Timothy's life, this specific gift that Paul is challenging him to fan into flame is the ability to preach the Word of God. We know this because in verses 1 and 2 of 2 Timothy, Paul says, "I charge you in the presence of God and of Christ Jesus, who is to judge the living and the dead, and by his appearing and his kingdom to preach the word, be ready in season and out of season; rebuke, exhort, correct, with complete patience and teaching." The gift was Timothy's ability and call to preach the Word.

Throughout the book of 2 Timothy, Paul reminds Timothy of people who were *not* living and preaching the Word. He mentions men like Hymenaeus and Philetus who had swerved from the truth and upset the faith of some people by saying that the resurrection had already happened. Paul instructs Timothy to continue to follow God's call for his life—preaching the word—without listening to these men. Just as Timothy learned to cultivate his gift, we must also discern our God-given gift and work to develop it for use in advancing the kingdom of God.

Consider Your Source

Paul's second exhortation to his protégé is this: *consider your source*. Friends, the only way we can fan into flame the gift of God is to trust in God as our source of power. Paul says, "for God gave us a spirit not of fear but of power and love and self-control." Now, I don't believe that Paul is suggesting that we can be overtaken by different spirits in the sense of an evil entity. Rather, I think Paul is describing the characteristics and the qualities of the Holy Spirit, one of which is *not* a spirit of fear. Gordon Fee thinks that the little "s" on "spirit" should be capitalized to a big "S" and that what Paul is describing is the work of the Holy Spirit in the Christian's life. What I believe Paul means is, "Timothy, the Holy Spirit is not fearful. He is powerful."

Don't forget that the Holy Spirit is a Person, the third Person of the Trinity. He is not an "It." He's not just a "Being." He is a Person. When you tap into the power of God by accepting Christ, God gives you the Holy Spirit. Paul describes this process in Ephesians 1:18: "I pray that the eyes of your hearts will be enlightened, that you may know what is the hope to which he has called you, what are the riches of his glorious inheritance in the saints."

The same power that God used to raise Jesus Christ from the dead empowers you and me as believers in Christ. Wow! Isn't that amazing? All the power of God has been given to us to use. When the Spirit enters your life, you're suddenly equipped with all this power. It is up to you to make the choice to use that power. Later in the book of Ephesians, Paul says that we can ask and God can do exceedingly above all that we ever ask or imagine according to this power that is at work within us.

In addition to power, we also have love. The word *love* that Paul uses is not the traditional word for love that you and I use. The Bible uses several different words for love. One type is *phileo* love, and another type is *agape* love. *Phileo* love is brotherly love. This type of love is transactional. For example, if you buy me a new car, then I will love you, right? That's transactional love. I love you because you gave me something of value.

But this is not the kind of love that is from God. This is more of a selfish love. In Matthew 6:5, Jesus says in essence, "Do not be like the hypocrites who stand on the street corners and who love to be heard for the words they say." That's a love that people get something in return for. That's *phileo* love. We could describe it this way: "If you love me, I will love you back."

Agape love, on the other hand, is unconditional. It's selfless and sacrificial. *Agape* is the kind of perfect love that God gives us. He loves us even when we can't love Him. Remember, Jesus says that He loved us first before we loved Him, and 1 John 4:8 reminds us that God is love. In John 15:13, Jesus says, "Greater love has no one than this, that someone lay down his life for his friends." Jesus laid down His life for His friends. In fact, He did more than that: He even went so far as to lay down His life for His *enemies.*

God's love is unchangeable. When Jesus was sharing the Last Supper with His apostles, scripture says that He loved them to the end. I can understand Jesus washing the feet of Peter and John, but do you realize that Jesus actually got down on His knees and washed the feet of Judas? Even knowing of Judas' disloyalty that would lead him to death, Jesus washed the feet of his betrayer. God's love is everlasting. Jeremiah 31:3 says that God's love is "an everlasting love." God's love is unfailing. First Corinthians 13:8 says, "Love never ends." God's love is unconditional—even to the point where He allowed His Son to die on the cross for us. Do you remember when Jesus called out from the cross, "Father, forgive them"? Why did He say that? "Because they do not know what they are doing." And finally, God's love is undeserved. Romans 5:8 says, "God shows his love for us in that while we were still sinners, Christ died for us."

As imitators of Christ, we are obligated to model this grace and forgiveness by loving the unlovable, just as Christ loved us. The only way we can truly love people who don't deserve our love is to surrender to the love of Christ as He works through us. The love of Christ *compels us* to love others.

If you love only yourself, focused on chasing your own desires, wants, and dreams, living life with only yourself in mind you'll never be able to love people the way God wants you to love them. You'll be too focused on yourself and your own needs and wants. When you choose to surrender to the Holy Spirit of God, He will give you His love. He will be the channel through which God will work and bear spiritual fruit in you.

Not only does the Holy Spirit give us power and love, but also self-control. This final Greek term means not just *self-control,* but *discipline.* When you surrender to the Spirit of God, He will give you discipline to control your body and your mind.

The question still remains: how are you and I able to fan into flame the gift that was given to us? How do we model courageous faith like Paul and Timothy did? This gift is something we didn't do anything to earn; it's something we don't deserve. How do we fan it? How do we rekindle our passion when it has dwindled to almost nothing?

We find a clue in chapter 1 verse 14. Paul says, "By the Holy Spirit who dwells within us, guard the good deposit entrusted to you." Later, Paul expands this idea in 2 Timothy 2:1 when he says, "You then, my child, be strengthened by the grace that is in Christ Jesus." He means, "Timothy, you're going to be strengthened from within by a power that is outside of yourself." Every day, you and I have to wake up and surrender to the Spirit of God, saying, "God, I can't do anything apart from You. Help me to fan my spiritual flame. Give me boldness and courage to share the gospel with others."

Scripture tells us that Paul anointed Timothy for ministry through the laying on of his hands. We don't know exactly how it happened, but 1 Timothy 4:14 says that all the elders gathered around Timothy Paul likely laid his hands on Timothy's head and spoke the words that the Lord led him to say. He may have said something like this: "Timothy, I know your father was not there for you the way you wanted him to be. But I'm your dad, Son. And I'm proud of you. You've been faithful. Your mother and grandmother have invested in you. You're going to do well for the Lord. I know you're shy and you don't think you can do it, but God's going to give you the power. I believe in you."

Can't you just imagine Timothy on his knees with tears running down his face as God spoke to him through Paul? Paul may have ended by saying, "Timothy, my son, preach the Word. Stand strong for the faith.

Be willing to suffer courageously for the gospel of the Lord Jesus Christ. Don't give up!"

Paul didn't lay hands on Timothy in order to fill him with more of the Holy Spirit. Like all believers, when Timothy chose to follow Christ, he received the Holy Spirit. Paul and the elders laid hands on Timothy in order to encourage him to give more of himself to the Holy Spirit. I often hear people say, "I just want more of God, more of God—give me more!" My friends, you don't need more of God; *God needs more of you.* When you come to Christ, you receive the Spirit of God and salvation (Romans 8:9). If you're a believer, you already have the Holy Spirit dwelling in you. You have all you need of God already. But He may need more of you!

So often, we forget that *we have resurrection power at our disposal.* If we choose to submit fully to the will of God, we will have much more power and boldness. I believe if Paul was standing here today, he would say the same thing to us: "what happened to the flame that was burning in your life many years ago—or just a few months ago? Fan it! Fan it! Pray. Depend on the Holy Spirit. Suffer courageously for the gospel. Take a stand in your home. Take a stand in your workplace. Take a stand in your city. Take a stand in your church. Fight the good fight. Run the race. Keep the course. Don't give up! Fan the flame!"

Now, listen to what Paul says in Ephesians 3:14: "For this reason I bow my knees before the Father, from whom every family in heaven and on earth is named, that according to the riches of his glory he may grant you to be strengthened with power through his Spirit in your inner being." There it is! The promise that you will be strengthened with power in your inner being by the Holy Spirit.

Paul prays for believers to be strengthened with power so that Christ may dwell in our hearts and cause us to be rooted and grounded in love. God wants us to comprehend the breadth, the length, the depth, and the height of Christ's love. He wants us to experience the love of Christ that surpasses knowledge, that we may be filled with all the fullness of the Holy Spirit.

Let's not forget that all power belongs to God. "Now to him who is able to do far more abundantly than all that we ask or think, according to the power at work within us, to him be glory in the church and in Christ Jesus throughout all generations, forever and ever. Amen" (Ephesians 3:20–21).

chapter 3

What Does Courageous Faith Look Like?

2 TIMOTHY 1:8-14

Y ou and I, as believers in Jesus Christ, are called to suffer well for the gospel. How? By knowing and trusting that our sovereign God is in control of all things. Courageous faith has at least three important qualities.

Paul writes in 2 Timothy 1:8–14:

> 8 Therefore do not be ashamed of the testimony about our Lord, nor of me his prisoner, but share in suffering for the gospel by the power of God, 9 who saved us and called us to a holy calling, not because of our own works but because of his own purpose and grace, which he gave us in Christ Jesus before the ages began, 10 and which now has been manifested through the appearing of our Savior Christ Jesus, who abolished death and brought life and

immortality to light through the gospel by the power of God, 11 for which I was appointed a preacher and apostle and teacher, 12 which is why I suffer as I do. But I am not ashamed, for I know whom I have believed, and I am convinced that he is able to guard until that Day what has been entrusted to me. 13 Follow the pattern of the sound words that you have heard from me, in the faith and love that are in Christ Jesus. 14 By the Holy Spirit who dwells within us, guard the good deposit entrusted to you.

Courageous Faith Stands in the Face of Suffering

We, like Timothy, have been given a responsibility for the sake of the gospel. As we examine the text, the first point I want you to see is this: *A courageous faith stands in the face of suffering.* In verse 8, Paul writes, "Therefore do not be ashamed of the testimony about our Lord, nor of me his prisoner, but share in suffering for the gospel."

The instruction for Timothy is that he suffer well. as he stands up for the cause of Christ. As I studied this passage, I asked myself, "Do we even know what suffering is? Do we have any clue what it means to really suffer for the sake of the gospel?" We live in a country where we're relatively free of persecution and suffering with regard to our belief in God and the gospel of Jesus Christ. But let me share with you Paul's wisdom and insight on the subject of what it means to suffer in Christ.

To do so, we must first look at Romans 8:16–17: "The Spirit himself bears witness with our spirit that we are children of God, and if children, then heirs—heirs of God and fellow heirs with Christ, provided we suffer with him in order that we may also be glorified with him." Likewise in 2 Corinthians 4:7–10, Paul is makes a case for suffering to the church at Corinth. He writes, "But we have this treasure in jars of clay, to show that the surpassing power belongs to God and not to us. We are afflicted in every way, but not crushed; perplexed, but not driven to despair; persecuted, but not forsaken; struck down, but not destroyed; always carrying in the body the death of Jesus, so that the life of Jesus may also be manifested in our bodies."

Paul acknowledges the crushing persecution being experienced by believers at the time, but reminds them that they will not be destroyed. This should serve as a reminder to those of us who feel as if we are persecuted or injured that we carry the death of Christ in our bodies so that people can see the light of Christ in our lives.

In Philippians 1:12, Paul says, "I want you to know, brothers, that what has happened to me has really served to advance the gospel so that it has become known throughout the whole imperial guard and to all the rest that *my imprisonment [my suffering]* is for Christ" (emphasis added). In other words, he is saying, "My present suffering is actually a physical example of the gospel to all who are watching me." We know that during his time in prison, Paul not only preached the gospel, but also lived the gospel by enduring suffering. His faith was so genuine that he was able to share the gospel with the very men who were causing his suffering.

Paul also writes in Philippians 1:29–30, "For it has been granted to you that for the sake of Christ you should not only believe in him but also *suffer* for his sake, engaged in the same conflict that you saw I had and now hear that I still have" (emphasis added).

In Colossians 1:24, Paul says, "Now I rejoice in my *sufferings* for your sake, and in my flesh I am filling up what is lacking in Christ's afflictions for the sake of his body, that is, the church" (emphasis added). Paul isn't rejoicing over the new house he purchased or the chariot he just bought. He is rejoicing in a time of extreme physical and mental anguish.

Finally, look at 2 Timothy 2:8–9. Paul writes to Timothy, "Remember Jesus Christ, risen from the dead, the offspring of David, as preached in my gospel, for which I am *suffering*, bound with chains as a criminal. But the word of God is not bound!" He continues in chapter 3, verse 12: "Indeed, all who desire to live a godly life in Christ Jesus *will be persecuted*" (emphasis added).

This may be hard for Christians in America to understand. When I look at the Western church, suffering is not a word that comes to my mind. The opposite is true. Compared to the standards of the world at large, many of us are living in the lap of luxury. In order to understand Paul's theology, we must view suffering from a global perspective. This involves two specific forms of suffering: *general suffering* and *gospel suffering*, or suffering persecution for the sake of the gospel.

General suffering is the kind of suffering you might experience on a normal day. On a small scale this suffering could mean that you didn't sleep well the night before a big meeting or that you woke up with a backache. Maybe a business deal went bad and you lost money, causing your family financial hardship. On a global scale, this suffering is seen in the devastation caused by war or natural disasters. This general suffering is a part of life that everyone experiences to different extremes.

Gospel suffering, on the other hand, happens when you are persecuted because you stood up for the cause of Jesus Christ. This suffering is for a reason, and those who maintain their faith and witness despite persecution will reap a great reward. Jesus told his disciples in John 15:18–19: "If the world hates you, know that it has hated me before it hated you. If you were of the world, the world would love you as its own; but because you are not of the world, but I chose you out of the world, therefore the world hates you 'A servant is not greater than his master.' If they persecuted me, they will also persecute you." This doesn't leave much room for interpretation, does it?

No healthy saint ever chooses suffering simply for the sake of suffering; he chooses to do God's will, as Paul did, whether or not it means suffering. In fact, Paul encourages Timothy in the face of suffering by saying, "Therefore do not be ashamed." That word *ashamed* is an interesting word. In the language of the New Testament, it's the word that means "undeserved humiliation."

We must be sure to draw a distinction between deserved and undeserved humiliation. Deserved humiliation is a result of sin or poor choices that we have made. We are humiliated for a reason. If a husband commits adultery against his wife, when he comes back to his wife and family trying to make ammends, he will face humiliation. And it is well deserved because of the sin he chose to commit.

Undeserved humiliation, on the other hand, may be more difficult to realize. Those who don't understand the gospel may see the humiliation of those who are persecuted for their faith as being appropriate. But Paul reminds us that one day we will not only realize our humiliation was undeserved, but we will be vindicated before all. In 2 Timothy 1:12 he says, "I'm not ashamed, for I know whom I have believed, and I am convinced that he is able to guard until that Day what has been entrusted to me."

Paul might explain it this way: "Timothy, I know you are being humiliated for the sake of the gospel now, but one day when Jesus Christ comes back, you will realize that all the humiliation you had on this earth was undeserved. When Jesus comes back, you will see that we are victors in the end! So there's no need to be ashamed about suffering for the gospel's sake. We're on the winning team." We are being commanded and encouraged to choose to associate ourselves with Christ, even in the face of suffering and persecution.

R. Kent Hughes says, "The theology of Paul's enemies was similar to the health-wealth and prosperity preachers of the day."[4] Hughes explains that in the first century, some people considered Paul's imprisonment and his sufferings in Rome to be shamefully unspiritual. They thought that Paul must have done something to earn God's disapproval. They saw his suffering as evidence that he was not of God. But Paul reminds Timothy that the gospel is not about having material wealth. It's not about achieving success in the world. The very essence of the gospel is standing up for the name of Christ, even if it means suffering.

It is as if he is telling us, "I don't want you to just share in suffering with me; I want you to lock arms with me. I want you to run headlong into suffering. Don't run away from it. I want you to embrace suffering if it means advancing the gospel of God."

Imagine the weight of these words as this young son in the faith heard from his spiritual father. He knew of the horrific torture and killing of Christ. He knew of Stephen's death from the eyewitness account of Paul himself. He most likely knew about the death and the beheading of James, John's brother. And here is his father in the faith telling him as he is chained in prison, "Don't be afraid or ashamed of suffering, Timothy. In fact, join me in suffering."

Most of us don't really know what Paul is talking about because we've never experienced this kind of suffering. But we are warned that when we decide to live a godly, moral life in Christ Jesus and stand up for our beliefs in the workplace, in our families, and in our neighborhoods, *we will suffer*. We need to know that when we stand up for the Lord, we're going to suffer. But our suffering is not anything compared to what is happening today, at this very moment overseas. Do you know that right now, millions of our brothers and sisters in Christ are suffering and dying for the faith?

I recently heard the story of a man named Ishtiaq Masih. Ishtiaq was a Christian man who went on a bus tour into Pakistan. The bus stopped on the side of the road. Ishtiaq walked up to a tea stall and picked up a bag of tea. Just as he was preparing to pay for the tea, the owner of the stall yelled at him to put down the tea. Shocked, Ishtiaq complied, but was confused by the owner's demands. Then he realized that the owner was pointing to a sign next to the tea stall that said, "If you are not a Muslim, you must confess your belief before you can buy anything." As Ishtiaq read the sign, the owner noticed that he was wearing a cross around his neck. The owner called for several other employees. A total of fourteen men ran over, and they hurled stones at Ishtiaq. They beat him with iron rods and clubs, and they stabbed him multiple times with kitchen knives as he pleaded for mercy.

Some of the others who had been on the tour bus rushed over to help Ishtiaq and were finally able to pull the attackers off of him. Ishtiaq was rushed to ICC Health Unit in Pakistan, but it was too late. The doctors said that he died from extensive internal and external injuries, brain damage, and a fractured skull.

It's a scary story, but attacks like this are happening all over the world today. Jesus tells His followers in Matthew 5:11–12, "Blessed are you when others revile you and persecute you and utter all kinds of evil against you falsely on my account. Rejoice and be glad!" Rejoicing in the face of suffering sounds impossible, but Jesus continues by telling us "your reward is great in heaven, for so they persecuted the prophets who were before you."

We should consider it an honor and privilege to suffer for Christ. According to Acts 5:41, as John and Peter left the prison in which they had been held, *they rejoiced that they had been counted worthy to suffer dishonor for the name of Christ*. Paul wanted to remind his son in the faith that when difficult times come—and they will come—he should not give up. Don't throw in the towel. Don't shrink back. Don't be weak or meek-minded. We, like Timothy, must press on courageously for the sake of the gospel of the Lord Jesus Christ.

It's easy to expect the Christian life to be a bed of roses. But we need to be reminded that we shouldn't give up when things don't go our way. Instead, we need to remember that not only should we expect suffering, we should anticipate it. And then when it happens in our lives, we won't get bent out of shape about it because we expected it, we anticipated it, we already locked arms with it, and we ran headlong into it for the sake of Jesus Christ.

I believe this is why Peter says the same thing in his first letter to the churches of the Diaspora in verse 20 of chapter 2: "For what credit is it if, when you sin and are beaten for it, you endure?" But if when you do good and suffer for it and you endure, this is a gracious thing in the sight of God." Being persecuted or punished for doing something wrong has no glory in it. But when you do good and you suffer courageously, God is pleased.

Peter concludes by saying, "For to this you have been called, because Christ also suffered for you, leaving you an example, so that you might follow in his steps." Jesus committed no sin; there was no deceit found in his mouth. When He was reviled, He did not revile in return. When He suffered, He did not threaten. But He continued entrusting Himself to the One who judges Him justly.

We serve the same God. It is our job to obey, serve, and please Him. And that's exactly what Paul is telling Timothy. He's saying, "Jesus suffered. I'm suffering. Timothy, you will suffer." My friends, you can expect to suffer when you stand up for the name of Christ. That's why the first element of courageous faith is this: we must stand in the face of suffering.

Courageous Faith Submits to the Sovereignty of God

In addition to standing in the face of suffering, *a courageous faith submits to the sovereignty of God.* Paul chooses this point in the letter to explain the gospel message "by the power of God, who saved us and called us to a holy calling, not because of our works but because of his own purpose and grace, which he gave us in Christ Jesus before the ages began."

Why does Paul do this? He wants to emphasize, first of all, that *it is God who saved us.* We don't have the ability to save ourselves. This reminds me of Ephesians 2:8–9: "For by grace you have been saved through faith. And this is not your own doing; it is the gift of God, not the result of works, so that no one may boast." That's the deal. It's God who does the saving.

Second, *God has set us apart.* He has saved us and called us to a holy calling. This sacred calling is directed from a holy God to a holy people to live a holy life and to be a holy nation.

Third, not only did God save us and set us apart, *He showed us Christ.* Verse 10 in the New International Version says, "it has now been revealed through the appearing of our Savior." Normally, the word *appearing* refers to the second coming of Christ. In the Bible, when you see a reference to Christ's appearing, it's normally referring to the time when He returns. However, that is not the case in this text. Here, Paul is actually talking about Jesus' initial act of coming to earth. And we know, as Paul did, that Jesus came for the purpose of abolishing death.

The term *abolish* is pregnant with meaning. In Greek, it means "to destroy." Jesus, when He died on the cross and rose again, rendered death inactive. He destroyed it. It's a word picture of someone facing an active bomb and disarming it so it doesn't have any destructive power left in it. That's what Jesus did by coming to earth. He abolished and disarmed death. That's why Paul writes in 1 Corinthians 15:54–57: "'Death is swallowed up in victory. O death, where is your victory? O death, where is your sting?' The sting of death is sin, and the power of sin is the law. But thanks be to God, who gives us victory through our Lord Jesus Christ."

Fourth, *God sent us.* He has a mission for each of us. He specifically chose Paul to be a preacher, a herald of the gospel. Paul was an apostle, commissioned by God for his particular mission. He was also a teacher. God entrusted him with an understanding of the fundamental doctrines of the faith. Paul tells Timothy, "Timothy, because God sent me, I'm suffering." Are you starting to see what's happening here?

God saved. God set apart. God showed. God sent. Now, notice the fifth and last point: *God will show up.* Paul writes that he is not ashamed, because "I know whom I have believed, and I am convinced that he is able to guard until that Day what has been entrusted to me." Aren't you looking forward to the day when Jesus Christ will vindicate the saints? When He will take all the wrongs and make them right? When He will create a new heaven and a new earth? Aren't you longing for the day when He will come back? Paul tells the church at Thessalonica in 1 Thessalonians 5:2, "For you yourselves are fully aware that the day of the Lord will come like a thief in the night."

Jesus Himself also teaches that while people are saying there is peace and security, then suddenly destruction will come upon them as labor pains come upon a pregnant woman., and they will have no escape. But we know that we, as children of the light, are not in the darkness and that day will not surprise us like a thief in the night.

These five points describing the gospel message may seem out of place, but I think Paul inserts the gospel right there as a reminder and demonstration to Timothy that God is in control of all things. If God did the saving and God did the sending and God does the setting apart and God does the showing and God will show up, then God must be the one who is in control.

Paul seems to be saying, "We're on the winning team, Timothy. We don't have to worry anymore because we're serving God, and on that day God will redeem our sufferings and vindicate the saints." He is teaching Timothy that the gospel is couched between sufferings. Look at verse 8: "Therefore do not be ashamed of the testimony about our Lord, nor of me his prisoner, but share in suffering." Then fast forward to verse 12: "But I'm not ashamed, for I know whom I have believed, and I am convinced that he is able to guard until that Day what has been entrusted to me."

"I am not ashamed," he says. It is clear that Paul is drawing a connection for Timothy between serving the Lord Jesus Christ by preaching the gospel and the suffering that will follow. We are being clearly shown that sharing the gospel with someone will mean suffering. The real question is: Are you suffering for the gospel?

For most of us, the answer is no. Maybe you're not sharing Jesus enough—or at all. If we aren't speaking up, we know we won't rock the boat. So we don't suffer because we choose not to talk about the gospel. We stay in our cubicle at work and we don't tell people about Christ.

But Paul wants to encourage Timothy to speak the gospel and to remember also that he will be persecuted for it. Because Paul and Timothy served the one who is control of all things, they knew that there was a reason for these things. Jesus says in Luke 12:4, "I tell you, friends, do not fear those who can kill the body, and after that have nothing more that they can do . . . fear him who, after he has killed, has authority to cast you into hell. Yes, I tell you, fear him!" God has the final authority, so we must follow Him no matter what.

Courageous Faith Safeguards the Gospel of God

When we choose to model courageous faith, not only will we stand in the face of suffering and submit to the Lord's sovereignty, we will also *safeguard the gospel of God*. Paul writes in verses 13–14 of 2 Timothy:

"Follow the pattern of sound words that you have heard from me, in the faith and love that are in Christ Jesus. By the Holy Spirit that dwells within us, guard the good deposit entrusted to you."

One way that we safeguard the gospel is by *following the words that we have heard*. In Greek, the word *safeguard* can mean "to protect," but it can also mean "to preserve." When you and I think of preserving something, we think of keeping it from spoiling. But the word *preserve* in the language of the New Testament is actually the word for "passing on." You see, in order to preserve something, we have to pass it on. Paul is telling Timothy, "Preserve the gospel by following the pattern of sound words and passing it on. You've heard the gospel from me. I've discipled you. I've taught you. I've spent time with you. Now pass it on."

Another way that we safeguard the gospel is *by the spirit we have*. Paul says that the security that was given to Timothy and to us, the church, is the gospel. Are you passing the gospel on to others every day?

Yes, when you share the truth, you will suffer. But Paul teaches us to share the sound words of the gospel "by the Holy Spirit who dwells within us." He says in verse 8, "Therefore do not be ashamed about the testimony of our Lord, nor of me his prisoner, but share in suffering for the gospel by the power of God."

If you want to stand up in the face of suffering, if you want to submit to the sovereignty of God, and if you want to safeguard the gospel, you have to do it by fanning into the flame this power within you. There is a difference between dynamite and *dunamis*—the Greek word for *power*. When dynamite goes off, there's an explosion and then it's over. But the word *dunamis* means a power that keeps exploding. It keeps going and going and going. Paul says, "You have an endless supply of power, Timothy. Fan into flame the gift of God, which is the Holy Spirit within you."

I think pastors need to stop promising riches and health and wealth and prosperity from the pulpits of Jesus Christ. Yes, those blessings are available to the believer in Christ. But pastors need to start promising that if you're going to follow the Lord Jesus Christ, you should not only expect suffering, you should anticipate it. And if you're not suffering, then I wonder how much and how well you're serving the Lord.

Let's be counted worthy to suffer well.

chapter 4

The Focus of a Life with No Regrets

2 TIMOTHY 1:15-18

Monasteries began with the assumption that if monks isolated themselves from other people, they would be able to better hear from God. If we were to do the same thing by isolating ourselves from others and shutting out the outside world, it might keep us from experiencing distractions and relational pain but it would not help us spread the gospel.

Because Paul wrote half of the New Testament, you may suspect that he was isolated from others due to the wealth of knowledge and spiritual wisdom that he possessed. It seems logical to think that he spent most of his time holed up in an ivory tower, studying the Word of God.

In reality, rather than isolating himself, Paul understood the importance of investing in others. He loved meeting new people and reuniting with old friends. Whether he was traveling with Silas, Barnabas,

John Mark, or Luke, or speaking words of encouragement to Timothy, Priscilla and Aquila, Paul enjoyed connecting with other people and spurring them on to greater faith in and obedience to Jesus Christ.

In the final chapter of Romans, Paul's closing remarks contain thirty-three names. Twenty-four of those people lived in Rome. What makes this truly amazing is that Paul hadn't even visited Rome yet. He had met most of those individuals through his travels, and they had taken up residence in Rome.

Paul loved people, but at the end of his life, he spent several years alone in prison. I want you to empathize with the pain that Paul feels as he spends his last few days on earth alone, isolated, and disappointed. He writes in 2 Timothy 1:15–18:

> 15 You are aware that all who are in Asia turned away from me, among whom are Phygelus and Hermogenes. 16 May the Lord grant mercy to the household of Onesiphorus, for he often refreshed me and was not ashamed of my chains, 17 but when he arrived in Rome he searched for me earnestly and found me—18 may the Lord grant him to find mercy from the Lord on that Day!—and you well know all the service he rendered at Ephesus.

Earlier in 2 Timothy, Paul wrote, "Therefore do not be ashamed about our Lord, nor of me his prisoner, but share in suffering for the gospel by the power of God." Paul was exhorting his son in the faith, "Timothy, be courageous in your faith. Don't cower down; I want you to be courageous in the face of suffering."

Notice what Paul does in verses 15 through 18. He gives us a visual illustration of the charge given to Timothy in verses 8 through 14. In order to teach Timothy about the kind of character he should possess, Paul contrasts two different types of people in verses 15 and 16. In verse 15, he says that everyone in Asia has turned away from him. He even mentions Phygelus and Hermogenes by name. In the next verse, he mentions one man, Onesiphorus, who was different. Onesiphorus was a faithful believer who refreshed Paul and was not ashamed of his chains.

Those Who Retreated from Paul

First, Paul gives an example of *those who retreated from him*. He begins by telling Timothy that everyone has deserted him. The New International Version says, "Everyone has left me." Now, although Paul literally says "all," we know this is not quite the case. Timothy was from Ephesus in Asia, and he didn't desert Paul. We know the household of Onesiphorus lived in Ephesus in Asia also, and they didn't desert Paul, either. So what was Paul saying? The impact of the two men who left him and the others who had turned their backs on him had left him feeling rejected and alone. He was isolated. He was saddened that the people he thought would stand up for him had run away. And Paul gives two names. By doing so, he is telling Timothy the two individuals who hurt him the most by failing to stand up for him.

Paul is not saying that since these men turned their back on him, they have apostatized the faith like Hymenaeus and Alexander in 1 Timothy. We don't know exactly what happened to these two men. We just know that they turned their backs on Paul. Many commentators believe that an event occurred in Paul's life that caused these two men to be afraid and desert Paul when the specter of suffering loomed.

I believe that event was Paul's arrest. He had arrived in Rome, excited to be there preaching the gospel. Then, all suddenly, the Roman guard came and grabbed him, put shackles on him, and dragged him away to prison. It seems that this is when Phygelus and Hermogenes decided to turn their backs on Paul for fear of being imprisoned or persecuted themselves.

Have you ever felt alone and isolated? Have you ever felt betrayed and let down by the very people you thought would always be there for you? We've all felt this way at times, disappointed in people and situations. One of the things I've learned about trials and tribulations in a person's life is this: your character and the strength of your faith will be revealed through times of testing. On whom are you really depending for strength: God or yourself?

It's easy for us to say, "I'm a believer in Jesus Christ" when everything is going well. It's easy to walk into church on Sunday morning and play the part of the good Christian. You can shine up on the outside. Put on a suit or a dress. Walk in holding a Bible. Wear a cross around your neck. It's easy to do that on Sunday. But how do you act on Monday around your coworkers? How do you act on Friday night when you get together with your friends? Do your family members, friends, and coworkers know you're a believer in Jesus Christ? What happens when pressure is applied to your life? Are you living for the Lord on the inside, or are you just shining up the outside to make yourself look spiritual?

Paul seems to feel that Phygelus and Hermogenes had put on an act. They seemed to be committed to following Christ. They acted like they would be there to support Paul in his ministry. But when times got tough, these two men said, "I'm out of here" and ran for the door.

Earlier in this book, I wrote about the difference between general suffering and gospel suffering. I showed you that general circumstances can happen in our lives to cause us to suffer, but certain types of suffering can also happen in our lives that will show people the gospel.

How you handle this suffering reveals your character. You're preaching the gospel in one way or another every day that you live. Everywhere you go, everything you say, every action, every thought, and every motive is representing the gospel to other people. That's why Paul says in Romans 5:3–4 that suffering builds character. He writes, "More than that, we rejoice in our sufferings" for we know" that suffering produces endurance, and endurance produces character, and character produces hope."

Likewise, James 1:2–4 says: "Count it all joy, my brothers, when you meet trials of various kinds, for you know that the testing of your faith produces steadfastness. And let steadfastness have its full effect, that you may be perfect and complete, lacking in nothing." James explains that how we handle suffering proves and develops our faith.

Saint Francis of Assisi said, "Go into the world and preach the gospel, and if necessary, use words." It's an interesting quote. But there's something missing theologically there, and that's this: in most cases, the gospel needs to be preached out loud in order for people to clearly understand it and respond to it. The Bible says that faith comes by *hearing*, and hearing by the word of Christ. People can't come to Christ unless they hear the gospel. The Good News has to be preached in order for a sinner to repent and turn to the Lord.

In Romans 10:14 Paul also asks us to consider how people will call upon the name of the Lord if they've never heard the gospel. How will they believe unless they hear? And how will they hear without a preacher? Someone has to preach the gospel so that they can hear the truth, so choose to believe, and call on the Lord.

Clearly, the gospel needs to be preached out loud. But Saint Francis also has a good point. As a believer, you are preaching the gospel everywhere you go and in everything you do, *even if you aren't saying a word.* Did you know that? If you profess to be a believer in Jesus Christ, you're preaching the gospel just by living.

The question is, what kind of gospel message are you preaching with your actions? What kind of life are you living? When you cower down in the face of suffering, you preach. When you say you believe in Christ but then live like you don't, you preach. When you say one thing but do another, you preach. What kind of message are you preaching today? Phygelus and Hermogenes definitely preached through their actions, but unfortunately, they preached the "gospel" of being cowards.

It may seem difficult to gain the holy boldness and courage we need to stand up for Christ, even in the face of suffering. But we do so by standing up next to believers in Christ and choosing to associate with godly people.

First Corinthians 15:33 (NIV) says, "Bad company corrupts good character." Sinful people will cause good people to sin. I'm not saying you shouldn't spend time with people who do not know the Lord. I'm not saying you shouldn't associate with non-Christians at all. This is what I'm saying: your best friends should not be lost people. Your best friends should be those who share your faith because the people you associate with will always influence you to be like them.

If you spend most of your time with friends who are alcoholics and hang out in bars, it doesn't take a rocket scientist to realize that you will probably begin to drink eventually. If you hang out with people who do drugs, at some point, you'll probably be tempted to start taking drugs yourself. If you hang around with guys at work who are cheating on their wives, it won't take long for you to begin to think about doing the same thing.

One thing I've learned from this passage is that spiritual cowards produce spiritual cowards. Just like Phygelus and Hermogenes, many of the other Christians in the area chose to desert Paul at a time when he needed them most. These men weren't loyal. When faced with a choice, they made the wrong decision. They checked out. It is this first group of people that I want to warn you about, But those who are spiritually courageous will produce others who are bold and courageous.

Those Who Remained with Paul

One of these courageous men, Onesiphorus, is mentioned by name in verse 16. He's different from the others who were frightened in the face of suffering. He cared enough to go and visit Paul in prison. He risked his own life to stand by Paul's side.

I see two defining characteristics in the life of Onesiphorus. The first is this: *Onesiphorus supported Paul through his attitude.* Paul says, "He came and he searched for me earnestly." That word "earnestly" in the language of the New Testament means "he looked long and hard" for Paul. He "looked high and low" for him.

There are three reasons that it was so difficult for Onesiphorus to find Paul. The first reason is that not only was Rome a massive city, it was a new city for Onesiphorus. It would be like if you went to New York City for the first time and tried to find one person without any contact information and with no access to the subway, a taxi, a bus, or a car. That's what Rome was like for Onesiphorus.

Second, it was hard for Onesiphorus to navigate through the city because he found out when he arrived that much of Rome had been burned by Nero. Remember that a couple of years earlier, the emperor Nero had burned down half the city and then blamed it on the Christians. So Onesiphorus was trying to find Paul in a city that had been destroyed and was in the process of being rebuilt. It may have looked like the cities in Haiti and other countries that have recently been devastated by natural disasters—destruction, filth, and the chaos of so many people made homeless.

Third and most important, Onesiphorus was not looking for the president of the country; he was looking for a man considered by Rome to be a criminal. Everywhere Onesiphorus went, he was trying to track down this "criminal." If you thought going to a new city and walking door-to-door and telling people about Jesus was difficult, just imagine going door-to-door trying to find a criminal. But Onesiphorus walked the streets day and night, knocking on doors, asking people, "Have you seen Paul?"

"Who?"

"Paul. Originally called Saul of Tarsus."

"No, we don't know him."

"Does anyone know about the apostle Paul around here?"

"No, never heard of him."

Onesiphorus looked long and hard for Paul. All the while, Paul was probably starving and wounded, sitting all alone with shackled hands and feet in a cold, dark, wet prison. But all of a sudden Paul hears a welcome voice,

"Hey, Paul. Is that you?"

"Yes, it's me."

"Finally, I found you! It's me—Onesiphorus." Can you imagine the joy Paul must have felt when he saw and heard or possibly even embraced his brother? He had been feeling so isolated and alone, but now this brother visited him, and Paul says, "He refreshed me." That word *refreshed* is connected in the Greek to the word *spirit*. What Paul is saying is, "He encouraged my spirit. He lifted me up."

Did you know that Christian fellowship with our brothers and sisters in Christ is a gift from God? That's why discipleship is so important to me and to the Lord. We need to be sharpened like iron, one to another, in a way that you won't find outside of a discipleship group. Paul says in the beginning of Romans, "To all those in Rome who are loved by God and called to be saints: Grace to you and peace from God our Father and the Lord Jesus Christ." Then in verse 11, he says, "I long to see you, that I may impart to you some spiritual gift to strengthen you." This gift is the mutual encouragement of believers through fellowship.

Onesiphorus was fiercely loyal to Paul. His example calls to mind a story about the loyalty of Alexander the Great's soldiers to their young leader. In 331 B.C., Alexander the Great was on track to take over the whole known world. He and his troops arrived at a certain area in India, and he brought his troops close to the high walls of a fortified city. As he approached the city, the king came to meet him. Alexander the Great marched up and said, "I am Alexander the Great, and I demand that you surrender immediately."

The king surveyed Alexander's troops and was less than impressed. He had many more troops in his city than Alexander had. These troops were also safely shut inside the city walls. There was no way for Alexander's troops to reach them. The king saw no reason to surrender.

Immediately, Alexander the Great lined up one hundred of his soldiers in a row, facing the edge of a nearby cliff and commanded them to march. One by one, they walked right to the edge of the cliff without hesitation. The first one walked off the edge and plunged to his death. The second one walked off right after him. Then the third one, and then the fourth. After eleven men had walked off that cliff in full view of the king, Alexander yelled, "Halt!"

The king was so stunned by the unflinching obedience of these men to their leader that he immediately surrendered. He knew that he could never win a battle against such loyal and disciplined soldiers. And Alexander the Great went on to conquer the entire known world.

I often wonder what it would be like if we, as followers of Christ, modeled that same fearless obedience. What would this world look like if we were loyal to Christ the way those soldiers were to Alexander the Great and the same way Onesiphorus was to Paul? What would the *church* look like? Very different, I'll bet.

Not only did Onesiphorus support Paul through his attitude, *he also supported Paul through his actions.* Paul equates the willingness of Onesiphorus to stand up for Paul with a willingness to stand up for Christ. I find an interesting similarity here between Paul's last days on earth and Jesus' last days on earth. Jesus Christ, before He went to the cross, informs His disciples, "You all will fall away from me." They were stunned.

Peter immediately defended himself in Matthew 26:33, saying that even if all the others fall away, he would never desert his Lord. Jesus only replied that Peter did not know what he was saying. Sure enough, Peter was in the courtyard when Jesus was brought before the high priest of the court. A young servant girl noticed that Peter was a Galilean and asked him if he knew Jesus.

He replied, "No, I don't know Him."

And then another servant girl said, "This man was with Jesus of Nazareth."

Peter denied it with an oath: "I do not know the man."

Then some other bystanders approached Peter and said, "You were with Jesus."

Again, Peter cursed and said, "I do not know the man."

Immediately the rooster crowed, and Peter wept bitterly when he realized that he has just denied Jesus three times.

When Jesus went to the cross, only one of His followers was brave enough to show up at the place of his crucifixion out of the twelve men He had discipled. This man was John, "the disciple whom he [Jesus] loved" (John 19:26).

Many years later, John wound being the last man standing too. Out of all the disciples, John was the only one who was not martyred. Could it be that because John was the one who met Jesus at the cross, the Lord spared his life and kept him from martyrdom? Every other disciple was martyred for the faith.

Let's return to the apostle Paul at the end of his life. Everyone has turned away from him. Onesiphorus is the only one left to refresh him. Isn't it amazing that just as John refreshed Jesus on the cross, Onesiphorus refreshed Paul at the end of his life?

We don't know for sure, but many commentators believe that Onesiphorus died very soon after he met with Paul. That could be why Paul says, "May the Lord grant mercy to the *household* of Onesiphorus" (emphasis added). If Onesiphorus had still been alive, Paul most likely would have said "May the Lord grant mercy to Onesiphorus."

R. Kent Hughes says, "If this view is correct, and Onesiphorus perished during his journey in taking care of Paul, perhaps it was due to the rigors of the ancient travel or even possibly to foul play in the Roman labyrinth."[5] In addition to that, Paul wrote "May the Lord grant him to find mercy from the Lord on that Day." He seems to be suggesting that Onesiphorus has already died and the next thing that will happen in his life is the second coming of Christ.

Other commentators believe that Onesiphorus was alive and that while he was on his way home, Paul sent this word to his family, apologizing for having kept Onesiphorus for so long and praying for blessings for their sacrifice.

Regardless, Onesiphorus was a man who sold out his life for the sake of Christ and risked everything to encourage Paul. And Onesiphorus was rewarded for his work by the honor given him by Paul. Yes, he may have died as a result of his visit to the apostle in prison, but Paul honored him. In Ephesus, people would have been talking about Onesiphorus throughout town. "Do you believe this guy? He risked it all to support the apostle Paul." What a great thing to be known for, right? And it was not only Onesiphorus who received honor, but his family, as well.

This man is remembered for being a man of great courage, so much so that in 2 Timothy 4:19, Paul writes, "Greet Priscilla and Aquila, and the household of Onesiphorus." Onesiphorus will always be remembered as a man of great courage.

On the other hand, there are two men who will always be remembered for something much less honorable. Phygelus and Hermogenes will forever be remembered for being cowards and refusing for stand up for their faith. They thought that insignificant act of turning away from the apostle Paul was no big deal. But their act is etched into the annals of eternity *forever* because the Word of God is forever, and for eternity they will be remembered as spiritual cowards.

It's one thing to be disgraced on earth, but it's another thing to stand face to face with the Lord Jesus Christ and have Him ask you, "Why did you turn your back on me?" That's what those two men will have to face.

One thing I appreciate about the apostle Paul is that although he made mistakes and even persecuted many Christians in his early days, he lived a life that was completely sold out to the Lord after his encounter with Jesus on the road to Damascus. He lived a life completely committed to the Lord with no regrets. For him, to live was Christ and to die was gain. Our goal should be the same.

When I think of other great men of the faith, one who comes to mind is Martin Luther, the great Reformer in Germany. Martin Luther was a Catholic monk who was riding on horseback when he had a transformational salvation experience. One of the bishops in the Catholic church sneaked him a Bible, and he began to read it. He stumbled across the passage in Ephesians 2:8–9 that says, "For by grace you have been saved through faith. And this is not your own doing; it is the gift of God, not a result of works, so that no one may boast."

When he read that, Martin Luther suddenly realized that it wasn't by his own goodness that he was saved; it was by the finished work of Jesus on the cross of Calvary. As soon as he realized this, he was radically converted. He became a professor at Wittenberg in Germany, and he began to teach people about the gospel. He began to write books. The real catalyst in his life was the day that he nailed his Ninety-five Theses on the door of the church in Wittenberg.

When the Catholic church heard of this and realized that Martin Luther was publicly opposing them, they called him to Rome. They put all his writings on a table for all to see, and they called him in. He was surrounded by the political elite. He was surrounded by corrupt religious leaders. Standing there all alone, he was asked this question: "Martin Luther, did you write these works?"

He said, "Yes I did."

They ordered him in front of all those people, "Recant, or you will die."

Luther requested a day to consider their demand.

He went back to his room where he was being held. His friends came to him and said, "If you do not recant, you will die. They'll kill you. You don't want to go out like this. Deny it. Martin, deny it!"

But after spending a day and a night in prayer, he went back to meet with the council. He stood up and said, "Unless I shall be convinced by the testimonies of the scripture or by clear reason, I neither can nor will make any retractions since it's neither safe nor honorable to act against one's conscience. Here I stand; I can do no other. God help me. Amen."

The religious leaders erupted in fury. They tried to take him into custody. They wanted to execute him. But as he traveled home on horseback, some of Luther's friends kidnapped him away from the authorities and brought him to a safe place. He lived in seclusion for many years, away from the Roman Empire. During that time he translated the Bible in the vernacular of the people.

Thanks be to God for Martin Luther. He was not ashamed to stand up against people who denied the deity of Christ in regards to being justified by faith through salvation. Additionally, they denied the sovereignty of God by selling indulgences and teaching people the theory of purgatory. Martin Luther stood up to those things, and because of that we're here today. He was able to live a life with no regrets.

How different history and our lives today would be if Martin Luther had been ashamed of the gospel of Christ and had recanted to preserve his own life?

We know how Phygelus and Hermogenes will be remembered. How will you be remembered? There's a very simple way to know whether or not you are ashamed of Christ. The next time you go to lunch with lost friends or people who don't know the Lord, stop for a moment before you eat and say, "Would you bow your head with me and pray to God? Everything we have comes from God, so I want to thank him for that." See if you are ashamed.

When you are with coworkers tomorrow or at work and you're talking about what you did over the weekend, why don't you stop and say, "Let me tell you about how God has changed my life"? See if you're ashamed.

Friends, let's start living out the truth that we believe.

chapter 5

How to Invest in the Lives of Others

2 TIMOTHY 2:1-2

Many Christians, including new believers in Christ and long-time followers of the Lord, have been given the wrong fuel for growth. The blame for this rests not on church members, but on the leaders of the church, specifically, the pastors.

The Southern Baptist Convention recently held a survey in which they asked Southern Baptist pastors, "What are the most important ministries in the church?" The results were not surprising. Pastors listed the ministry of outreach, the ministry of evangelism, the ministry of the worship service on Sunday morning, and the ministry of Sunday School classes as the most important ministries in the church. All of those things are good. But the ministries of discipleship and prayer came in last on the list. Discipleship rated a paltry 7 percent, and only 5 percent of pastors listed prayer as an important ministry of the church. And we wonder why 85 percent of Southern Baptist churches are at a plateau or are declining in attendance! We're neglecting two of the most fundamental ministries of the church.

Bill Hull says, "It's puzzling that putting disciple-making at the center of our ministry is tough, even though Jesus Christ left us with a clear imperative to go and to make disciples."[6] Jesus left us with a command. It's not an option. It's not a multiple choice question. He said, "Go and make disciples."

Jesus Christ didn't come to earth to promote a program; He came with a plan. That plan was to make disciples. In fact, in the entire New Testament, the word *Christian* is only used three times. Two of those times, it is used as a derogatory term. Only in the more recent past has it become an honor to be called a Christian.

On the other hand, the word *disciple* is used in the New Testament 269 times. It appears 238 times in the Gospels alone. It seems to me that Jesus wants disciples more than he wants Christians. Being a disciple is not just about walking down the aisle on Sunday morning, raising your hand in the service, or signing your name on a card. A disciple is somebody who follows, who learns, who grows.

When you stop and think about yourself and all of the Christians around you, how many people are true disciples of Christ in the way that God intended? I have a sneaking suspicion that the number is very few. That's why Paul challenges Timothy, in this last letter to his spiritual to not only make more disciples but to teach other people how to make disciples, as well.

Let's take a look at 2 Timothy 2:1–2.

> 1 You then, my child, be strengthened by the grace that is in Christ Jesus, 2 and what you have heard from me in the presence of many witnesses entrust to faithful men who will be able to teach others also.

This is one of the texts that inspired Dr. Billy Graham to spend his life sharing the gospel and making disciples. He said, "One of the first verses of Scripture that Dawson Trotman, the founder of Navigators, told me to memorize was 2 Timothy 2:2. This is like a mathematical formula for spreading the gospel and enlarging the church."[7]

If pastors truly want to grow their churches, they should not invest in programs; they should invest in people. Paul taught Timothy, Timothy shared the truth with faithful men, and these faithful men then went out and taught others also. And so the process continues on.

Billy Graham also said, "If every believer followed this pattern, the church could reach the entire world in one generation. The mass crusades in which I believe and to which I have committed my life will never accomplish the Great Commission; one-on-one ministry will."[8] That's pretty amazing!

In just these few opening verses Paul has given Timothy a process for making disciples (verses 1 and 2) and a picture of what discipleship should look like. In this chapter, we're going to explore the process of discipleship. Keep in mind that the overarching theme here is that *God is calling you and me to be empowered disciple-makers.*

Abide in the Power of Christ

In order for us to be empowered to make disciples, *we must first abide in the power of Christ.* Paul writes, "You then, my child, be strengthened by the grace that is in Christ Jesus." We cannot do anything in the Christian life apart from God's grace that is found only in Christ Jesus. The word *strengthened* in the Greek New Testament means "empowered by" or "to be made strong" in order to accomplish a task. The use of the present tense for this word implies that being strengthened is something that must occur every single day. The term is also in the passive voice, which means that the subject is not performing the action but receiving the action.

Paul is essentially telling Timothy, "The way you will be strengthened for ministry and discipleship is by relying on God's grace." The good thing about God is that His grace never ends. He gives grace upon grace; He gives energy and power. We choose to rely on God's grace by meditating on God's Word and His character, by thinking about God's grace, by asking God to give us grace, and by waiting patiently to receive His grace.

Remember that Paul tells Timothy in chapter 1, verses 6–7, "For this reason I remind you to fan into flame the gift of God, which is in you through the laying on of my hands, for God gave us a spirit not of fear but of power and love and self-control." In verses 13–14, he says, "Follow the pattern of sound words that you have heard from me, in the faith and love that are in Christ Jesus. By the Holy Spirit who dwells within us, guard the good deposit entrusted to you."

This is a reminder that the Christian life is an upside-down kingdom. It's radically different from the kingdom of this world. You don't gain strength by acting in your own power; you gain strength by waiting on the Lord.

Let's look at a related biblical principle from the words of Jesus. In John 15:4–5, Jesus says, "Abide in me, and I in you. As the branch cannot bear fruit by itself, unless it abides in the vine, neither can you unless you abide in me. I am the vine; you are the branches. Whoever abides in me and I in him, he it is that bears much fruit, for apart from me you can do nothing." Did you catch that? Apart from Jesus, we can do *nothing*. As Christ works in us, He also works through us.

Second Corinthians 12:7–10 is one of my favorite passages. In these verses we see Paul describing a thorn in the flesh, or messenger from Satan, sent by God to keep Paul from becoming conceited regarding the greatness of the revelations God had made to him. Three times Paul pleaded with the Lord to remove this torment. But God refused, reminding Paul, "My grace is sufficient for you, for my power is made perfect in your weakness." Paul responds, "Therefore I will boast all the more gladly in my weakness so that Christ's power may rest on me." Paul tells us that the power of Christ rests on him when he boasts in his own weaknesses, insults, hardships, and persecutions. He knows that it is only when he is weak that he can be strong in Christ. To be strengthened by Christ is to be weak, humble, and open to His leading.

The one issue in your life that can seriously hinder the work of Christ is your pride. Humility, on the other hand, says, "I can't do this in my own strength. I need Christ." That's why James 4 tells us that God opposes the proud but gives grace to the humble.

If you are not reading the Word of God, I can guarantee you that you are not experiencing the fullness of the grace of God that should be given to you through the Word. One of the main facets of discipleship is having a regular quiet time with the Lord. If you're not drinking deeply from the well of His Word, how else can God deliver his grace and strength to you?

Accept the Principles of Christ

We must not only abide in the power of Christ, but we must also *accept the principles of Christ*. Paul tells Timothy to pass on "what you have heard from me in the presence of many witnesses." The word *witness* here actually means, "martyr." It's the word for someone willing to die for his or her faith.

Paul is saying, "You can test what I'm saying by the witnesses. These men don't just speak the Word or listen to the Word; these men are going to die for the Word of God. They are not just church attendees; these men are literally willing to die for their faith in the Lord Jesus Christ."

It's one thing to stroll into church on Sunday morning and hear an uplifting word from God through the pastor. It's another thing to live faithfully from Monday through Saturday. Are you putting the words you hear on Sunday into your life? Paul wanted to be sure that Timothy didn't just hear the Word, but applied it faithfully to his life.

Deuteronomy 4:1 (NIV) says, "Hear now, O Israel. The decrees and the laws I am about to teach you. Follow them so that you may live." And in Deuteronomy 5:1 (NIV), Moses summons all of Israel and says,

"Hear, O Israel, the decrees and laws I declare in your hearing today. Learn them and be sure to follow them."

Scripture always makes a strong connection between hearing and doing. But there is a heresy being taught in churches today. It's reflected in this attitude: "I can choose to get saved by Jesus today but put off obedience to Him until I die and go to heaven, right? Hey, I don't really want to be like Jesus! I just want fire insurance, pastor. I just don't want to go to hell." I'm sorry, friends, but you cannot choose Jesus as Savior without choosing Him as Lord of your life. You have to follow Him and obey Him if you want to choose Him as Lord.

Recently, I spoke to a youth group, and I told the students, "You don't have to tell me what you believe; just let me watch what you do and I'll tell you what you believe. Your life will prove (or disprove) the case for the faith you attest to. The way you live will show me if you are a believer or a disciple in Jesus Christ."

Before you can make disciples, you've got to be a disciple. Are you a true disciple of Christ in the sense of the word that Jesus meant? If you are, then you can move on to the next step.

Invest in the People of Christ

A disciple is someone who *invests in the people of Christ*. Paul writes to Timothy, "And what you have heard from me in the presence of many witnesses entrust to faithful men who will be able to teach others also."

In this verse, Paul gives Timothy a command. It's not an option; it's not a choice. *Entrust. Disciple.* Timothy had been given a gift and Paul wanted to be sure he realized that the only way to safeguard and protect the gospel was by giving it away.

If God has worked in your life, you need to give the investment away. The goal of Christianity is not to show up at church every Sunday morning and simply be fed by the pastor; the goal of Christianity is to be fed in a way that allows and encourages you to *give it away*. Are you giving it away?

Think of the Christian life as being a metal chain made of individual links. Every Christian is either connecting links or breaking links in the chain. You are either making connections, discipling people, and passing the baton to others in the faith or you're breaking links. And that destroys the chain.

Who are we supposed to invest in? Paul says, "faithful men." Unfortunately this doesn't apply to everyone because not every wants to be disciple. In many churches, probably less than half of the attendees really want to be discipled. They are happy simply showing up at church on Sunday morning and staying in a comfortable spiritual place.

In the seven-and-one-half years that I've discipled men in my ministry and my life, I've only seen half of them continue the spiritual journey for the long haul. I think that Paul is emphasizing the need for Timothy to find men who have a heart for God and a passion to not only make disciples, but also to be discipled.

Sometimes we think Jesus had only twelve followers to choose from, but the truth is that He had to turn away more men that he chose. Jesus had thousands of men to choose from. Of the thousands who wanted to follow Him, He had to choose twelve who would be devoted to the cause.

He had to exclude many men, and I'm sure a lot of them were faithful. Jesus did not pick His disciples because they knew everything or because they were wealthy, brilliant, well-schooled, or talented theologically. Far from it! I believe that the one characteristic Jesus looked for in His disciples was that *these men were teachable.*

I can work with somebody if they only have one talent, but I cannot work with them if they don't have the characteristic of being teachable. In fact, you can even have little talent but still be teachable, and I can work with you. We must to get to the place where we desire to grow and learn. Paul writes in 1 Corinthians 3:1–2: "Brothers, I could not address you as spiritual people, but as people of the flesh, as infants in Christ. I fed you with milk, not solid food, for you were not ready for it. And even now you are not yet ready, for you are still of the flesh."

Let's grow up and mature from being infants to those who are ready for solid spiritual food.

John Wesley, the great evangelist, said, "Give me a hundred men who fear nothing but God, hate nothing but sin and are determined to know nothing among men but Jesus Christ and him crucified, and I will set the world on fire with them."[9] Do you realize that if the apostles had only evangelized and hadn't discipled anyone, none of us would be here today? Think about it. The call to faith is a call to teach people to pass on the gospel and the legacy of Christ.

What if twelve of us had been chosen to be the twelve apostles? Would you and I be able to pass the message on for thousands of years? The weight of that responsibility rested upon those men.

Paul discipled elders and deacons and prophets and leaders of the church. Eventually, he discipled Timothy. He tells Timothy, "You've been invested in; now go and make an investment in another person. Not in a 401(k), not in any retirement plan; invest in people. That's the only way your legacy is going to live on: by investing in people."

I would rather invest in a thousand people who become faithful followers and disciples of the Lord Jesus Christ than have a church of five thousand people who are a mile wide and an inch deep. I believe we can change our cities; I believe we can change the world. I love preaching, but this kind of change is not going to happen by preaching alone. We must invest in people.

Repeating the Purpose of Christ

The last piece of the puzzle is *repeating the purpose of Christ*. Jesus Christ was adamant about making disciples. Not making disciples wasn't an option for Him; He came to the earth with a mission. That's why Paul says, "What you've heard from me in the presence of many witnesses entrust to faithful men who will be able to teach others also." In this text, we see four generations of discipleship. I love that! Paul taught Timothy; that's one to two. Timothy is instructed to teach faithful men;

that's two to three. And those faithful men are instructed to teach others also. We find four generations of disciples mentioned in this one verse. What a challenge to us today!

How many people have you personally disciple and invested in who are now repeating the process in others? You see, when the church becomes an end in itself, it ends. When Sunday School, as great as it is, becomes an end in itself, it ends. When small groups ministry becomes an end in itself, it ends. When the worship service becomes an end in itself, it ends. What we need is for discipleship to become the goal, and then the process never ends. The process is fluid. It's moving. It's living. It's active. It must continue to go on.

Every Christian could be compared to one of two bodies of water: the Jordan River or the Dead Sea. The Jordan River is an active body of water. It flows from north to south. The Dead Sea, on the other hand, only has one inlet and no outlets. Water comes in from the north to the lowest point in the world, and it doesn't flow back out. So the water is stagnant; it just sits there. I believe that all Christians are like these bodies of water. You're either flowing and moving as God uses you to impact the lives of other people or you're stagnant and lifeless, like the Dead Sea.

In John chapter 17, we find Jesus' mission for coming to the earth, in addition to dying and rising from the dead to redeem our sins. This chapter contains the last prayer that Jesus lifts up to the Father. He asks in essence, "Father, if there is any way, let this experience pass from Me; yet not My will, but Your will be done."

At the beginning of this prayer, Jesus offers us an interesting insight into His mission. In John 17:4, He addresses God the Father, saying, "I glorified you on earth, having accomplished the work that you gave me to do." Rather than *accomplished*, another Bible version says *finished*. I love that word. Finished. It's the same word that Jesus uses on the cross when He says, "It is finished!"

Jesus knew that the task God sent him to accomplish was complete, and He says this to acknowledge that he has done what He came to do.

You might assume that the task given to Jesus was to go to the cross and die for the sins of mankind. That's true, but here Jesus is saying, "It's finished," and He had not gone to the cross yet. So what was the task that Jesus was supposed to do that He had already accomplished?

Leroy Eims writes, "When you read this prayer in chapter 17, you'll notice that He did not mention miracles or multitudes one time; but he mentions forty different times the men whom God gave Him out of the world."[10] These men that He mentions are the disciples He invested in during His time on earth. In verse 6, He says, "I have manifested your name to the *people* whom you gave me out of the world. Yours *they* were, and you gave *them* to me, and *they* have kept their word" (emphasis added).

Jesus Christ was interested in making disciples. That's why He commanded His followers to "go and make disciples." You may be tempted to say, "Well, I'm not a pastor. I'm not a teacher." You don't have to be a pastor or a teacher to disciple people. You don't have to be a pastor or a teacher to join a discipleship group. The great thing about discipleship is that it's not just you teaching others; it's other people teaching you. It's accountability. It's encouragement. It's fellowship between one believer and another.

After my first discipleship meeting over lunch, I'll never forget what one of the guys told me. He looked at me and said, "Robby, I never knew that I could be discipled. I grew up in church all my life, and I've never known that it was even an *option* for me to be discipled. My view of Christianity was that I should come in on Sunday, hear a word from the Lord, and then try all week to pull myself up by my own bootstraps, and then come back the next Sunday and go out and do it again." He also told me, "I didn't realize that somebody could come alongside of me and teach me how to pray, teach me how to memorize scripture, teach me how to love my wife, teach me how to serve my church, and teach me how to serve the Lord and love it. I didn't know that was even possible."

I have a feeling that many of you may not be aware that discipleship is an option either. Discipleship is about getting together with two or three men or two or three women and saying, "Hey, let's study the Bible together. Let's learn together. Let's grow together. Let's see God work in our lives." My goal for the people in my own church is for every person—whether he or she is a leader, a staff member, a Sunday School teacher, a nursery worker, a church member, a visitor, a member of the choir, a deacon, or anything else—to disciple another person or be discipled by someone at all times.

I'd like to see the youth discipling the younger children, the college students discipling the youth, the young adults discipling the college kids, the middle-aged adults discipling the young adults, and the senior adults discipling the middle-aged adults. This is how the process of discipleship should work. Can you imagine how different the church would look if we did this? People would say, "Man, there's something different about those Christians. They really care about other people. They invest in the lives of people."

I once heard a story about Jesus going into heaven after His work on earth was over. As He entered heaven, all of the angels were there waiting for Him. They asked Him this question: "Jesus, how are You going to get Your salvation plan out into the world?"

Jesus looked at them and said, "I've already left it in the hands of the disciples."

One of the angels asked, "What if they fail?"

Jesus said, "We have no other choice. That's it."

We're His disciples. Let's pass on God's truth to others.

chapter 6

Leaving a Legacy
of Eternal Impact

2 TIMOTHY 2:3-7

What kinds of spiritual activities should a true disciple of Christ engage in? We need to answer that question in order to discover what an obedient disciple (and an effective disciple-maker) looks like. Let's explore the portrait of discipleship Paul draws for us in Timothy in 2 Timothy 2:3–7:

> 3 Share in suffering as a good soldier of Christ Jesus. 4 No soldier gets entangled in civilian pursuits, since his aim is to please the one who enlisted him. 5 An athlete is not crowned unless he competes according to the rules. 6 It is the hard-working farmer who ought to have the first share of the crops. 7 Think over what I say, for the Lord will give you understanding in everything.

Most commentators believe that in this passage, Paul presents the following four metaphors for the Christian life: a teacher (verse 2), a soldier (verse 3), an athlete (verse 5), and a farmer (verse 6). Yes, there are metaphors in the text, but I differ with many commentators because I believe Paul uses only three metaphors here.

If Paul were trying to tell us that we should literally be these four things, we would expect them to be in the form of commands. For example, "Timothy, you need to be a teacher. You need to be a soldier. You need to be an athlete. You need to be a farmer." But that's not how the imperatives (commands) operate in the text. We find four imperatives in the opening of chapter two, but they are different from the metaphors.

Let's look again at verses 1 and 2, which we studied in the previous chapter: "You then, my child, be strengthened by the grace that is in Christ Jesus, and what you have heard from me in the presence of many witnesses entrust to faithful men who will be able to teach others also."

Paul uses the first imperative or command in verse 1: *strengthen*. The second command is found in verse 2: *entrust*. The third appears in verse 3: *suffer*. And the fourth one is found in verse 7: *understand*. The overarching theme of 2 Timothy 2:1–7 is disciple-making. The first two verses give us the context or the principle of discipleship, and the next four verses paint a picture of how true discipleship looks.

I also believe that while Paul gives four imperatives in this passage, there are only three, metaphors. Since Timothy is literally a teacher, I don't think the example of teaching and entrusting is a metaphor. In verses 4 through 7, Paul depicts the disciple-maker as the suffering soldier, the strict athlete, and the steadfast farmer. Paul uses these word pictures to show Timothy that the main goal of his ministry should be to make disciples. And the main goal for every believer in Jesus Christ is to make disciples. That's the mission we've been given, and our mission never changes.

The Suffering Soldier

In the first metaphor, found in verse 3, Paul calls Timothy to be like *a suffering soldier for the advancement of the gospel*. He says, "Share in suffering as a good soldier of Christ Jesus." Paul does not simply mean for Timothy to endure suffering, in the sense of putting up with it. Paul is urging Timothy to willingly join and share in his own sufferings.

The main thing that we need to be fighting for as believers in Jesus Christ is to preserve the gospel. The gospel message is that God sent His Son to earth, wrapped in human flesh, to live and die and be resurrected and ascend into heaven as the atoning sacrifice for our sin. His death in our place satisfied God's wrath, gives us access to the living God, and allows us to have eternal life and, amazingly, to be filled with the Spirit of God today.

As a believer in the Lord Jesus Christ, when you stand up for the gospel, you are going to be attacked. You have to be ready as a soldier. You see, a soldier doesn't have a regular day job. He doesn't work nine to five with an hour off for lunch. He doesn't punch a time card. He doesn't get weekends off to do whatever he wants. He doesn't get paid holidays or sick days. A soldier is a soldier twenty-four hours a day, seven days a week; his life is not his own. When he enlists in the army, he gives up his rights to do whatever he wants.

Listen to what Paul says: "No soldier gets entangled in civilian pursuits." I love that word *entangled*. It means "to be intertwined with"; it means "to be mixed together with." Paul is telling Timothy that as a soldier of the Lord Jesus Christ, he must stay focused on the task at hand. Paul isn't saying that you can't associate with former friends or that you can't go to former places, but he is saying that your lifestyle should be bent toward God. When people look at your life, they should not see that you are more entangled in civilian pursuits than in the task at hand, which is to serve the Commander in Chief above all else.

Of course, getting us entangled in civilian pursuits is what the devil tries to do at all costs. If the devil can get our minds off of God and onto petty things, he wins. The Bible says that Satan comes to steal, kill, and *destroy*. In fact, if you study the book of Ezekiel, you'll find that Lucifer was cast out of heaven because he tried to get the angels to stop focusing on the worship of God and to start following him. In his prideful heart, he wanted to become greater than God.

Sometimes the petty arguments, issues, and frivolous concerns that we focus on may just be our personal preferences. We need to watch ourselves to make sure we are about the business of making the advancement of the gospel of the Lord Jesus Christ the main thing in our lives. We do this by glorifying God in everything we do, which includes making disciples of other people and teaching them how to do the same. That is the main reason we have been enlisted into service as soldiers of the Lord Jesus Christ.

When I hear a person say, "Pastor, I prefer it when you do things this way," or "I think of it this way," I am concerned. The gospel is not about what you or I like or prefer. That's why Paul warns Timothy not become entangled in such things as frivolous arguments that arise in the church." He says in 2 Timothy 2:14–15: "Remind them of these things, and charge them before God not to quarrel about words, which does no good, but only ruins the hearers. Do your best to present yourself to God as one approved, a worker who has no need to be ashamed, rightly handling the word of truth."

The emphasis here is on our job as believers to please the One who enlisted us. Like Timothy, we should be consumed only with following Jesus. When we take our focus off of Jesus and start focusing on our-selves, that's when we start to struggle.

This passage that depicts the stoning of Stephen, Acts 7, serves as an excellent example of how our lives should be focused. Up to this point, most of the apostles were still living in Jerusalem and the surround-ing area of Judea; they hadn't taken the gospel beyond that area. Ste-phen, one of the followers of Christ, was questioned before the religious leaders and the corrupt politicians of that day. He answered with an eloquent presentation of the gospel.

After Stephen spoke, "They were enraged, and they ground their teeth at him." But we see in Acts 7:55: "But he, full of the Holy Spirit, gazed into heaven and saw the glory of God, and Jesus standing at the right hand of God."

Notice that Jesus is not sitting anymore; He is standing at the right hand of God. Then Stephen said, "Behold, I see the heavens opened, and the Son of Man standing at the right hand of God." The people cried out with a loud voice and stopped their ears and rushed together at him. Then they cast him out of the city and stoned him. A young man named Saul (or Paul) was responsible for watching the garments of those casting the stones. As they stoned him, Stephen called out, "Lord Jesus, receive my spirit." Falling to his knees, he cried with a loud voice, "Lord, do not hold this sin against them." Then he went to be with his Creator. Isn't it interesting that two of the things Stephen said ("receive my spirit" and "do not hold this sin against them") remind us of the words that Jesus says from the cross?

Acts chapter 8, verse 1 says, "And Saul approved of his execution. And there arose on that day a great persecution against the church in Jerusalem, and they were all scattered throughout the regions of Judea and Samaria, except the apostles."

After Stephen's death, the people began to persecute those who believed in the Lord Jesus Christ. Because of the intense persecution, the Christians were forced to scatter. Imagine if somebody began attacking Christians in your community and you and your fellow church members began to fear for your lives. You might say, "I'm going out west ," or "I'm moving north."

Acts 8:4 says, "Now those who were scattered went about preaching the word." That word *scattered* is the word for sowing seed. Those who were persecuted were sown like seeds out into the world in order to grow and bear fruit. God used persecution in the lives of these believers to help spread the gospel.

This leads us to a profound truth: you preach the gospel the best when you are persecuted the most. We live in a world where many pastors think they have to try to make the gospel relevant to people. But the lost world is not looking for something relevant; they're looking for something real. Non-Christians want to know that your faith will last even in the face of the worst of life's troubles, trials, and persecution. They want to know that it's real. God's Word says that there's no better way to spread the gospel than to send persecution into the lives of believers.

In Acts 11:19, we find that "those who were scattered because of the persecution that arose over Stephen traveled as far as Phoenicia and Cyprus and Antioch, speaking the word to no one except Jews." Did you ever think about the fact that your present trials and persecution may be empowering you to preach the gospel to your friends? In fact, it may be the only gospel they ever hear. My challenge to you is this: don't run from persecution anymore. Ask God to be glorified through your persecution as if you were a suffering soldier.

The Strict Athlete

Paul then exhorts Timothy to be like *a strict athlete* (verse 5). He writes, "An athlete is not crowned unless he competes according to the rules." Athletics back in the first century were extremely competitive. Paul would have been very familiar with the Greek games.

In order to participate as an athlete in these games, you had to qualify in three areas. First, you had to be Greek by birth. You couldn't compete in the Greek games unless you were a native-born Greek.

Second, you had to train competitively. By oath, you had to commit to training strenuously for ten straight months. Then, before the games, you had to stand before the statue of Zeus in front of all of the spectators, and say, "I have committed to ten straight months of disciplining my body for the games." The Athenians didn't want any slackers to compete in the games. They wanted people who were disciplined, people who could go the distance.

Third, if you wanted to compete, you had to abide by the rules. For example, if you were competing in a long-distance run, you couldn't take shortcuts through the city; you had to stay on the agreed-upon course or you would be disqualified.

Now think of the parallels to the Christian life. In order for us to be a part of the team, we have to be born again by trusting in the Lord Jesus Christ for salvation. God also says that you have to compete according to the rules. There are certain rules and commandments by which He wants you and me to live. In addition to that, you should be disciplining your spirit, mind, and body. That's what Paul we learn from Paul in 1 Timothy 4:8: "While bodily training is of some value, godliness is of value in every way, as it holds promise for the present life and also for the life to come."

The Christian life is like a relay race. John MacArthur tells a story about a time when he was running track in college. He was one member of a four-man team that ran the 4 X 100-meter relay race. He and his teammates had trained for months to make it to the state competition. At the state finals, after the gun went off, the first teammate started running. He was on pace to run one of his best times in the relay. After MacArthur was handed the baton, he went on to run one of his best times ever. His team was in first place as he passed the baton to the third teammate, who.grabbed it and started running.

Halfway through the last lap, the third teammate decided to quit. Right in the middle of his leg of the race, he stopped running and simply started strolling off the track onto the infield.

MacArthur and his other teammates thought, "Man, the worst possible thing must have happened to him. He must have pulled a hamstring, or God forbid, he broke his ankle." So MacArthur ran over to his buddy and asked, "What happened?"

His teammate said, "I don't know, John. I just don't feel like running anymore."

"You just don't *feel* like running?" MacArthur asked incredulously.

"Yeah, I just don't feel like running."

The coach came over. You can imagine how enraged he and the rest of the team were. That guy had let down not only the coach, but the students, his fellow athletes, and his school. He had disgraced the school.

The coach told him, "Don't you know that you're not just representing yourself, but you're representing your team and your school here? What about all the time that I invested in you? What about your teammates? How could you, in one brief, selfish second, destroy all of that?"

When you and I hear that story, we think, "How in the world could that guy do that?" But the truth is that there are leaders in the church today who are walking away from the gospel ministry, saying, "I just don't want to run anymore." Churchgoing people who have been Christians for years are walking away and saying, "I'm tired. I just don't want to run anymore."

That's why Paul is emphatically telling Timothy, "Listen to me. You're going to be tempted to give up. You're going to feel like throwing in the towel. Don't give up! This is not your race alone; God has called you to this race. God has called you into this competition. Timothy, stay strong. Run the good race. Fight the good fight. Keep the faith. Don't give up!"

I have a feeling that some of you reading this may be holding onto your faith by a thread. Pain, discouragement, disillusionment, failed relationships, and other factors have brought you to the point where you feel like throwing in the towel. My charge for you today from the Word of God is this: don't give up! Listen, this isn't your race; God has called you to represent Him. I'm not talking only to pastors and leaders and teachers and ministers; I'm talking to you. I'm talking to the people of God. Don't give up!

The Steadfast Farmer

Finally, God has called us to be like *a steadfast farmer.* Paul writes, "It is the hard-working farmer who ought to have the first share of the crops."

He uses the term *hard-working* to describe ministerial labor. *Hard-working* means to work, to toil, until you can toil no more; to sweat until you can sweat no more; and to continue working and serving until you're spent.

Paul uses the same word in 1 Timothy 5:17 when he says, "Let the elders who rule well be considered worthy of a double honor, especially those who *labor* in preaching and teaching" (emphasis added). Did you know that it's hard work to stand up every Sunday and preach the Bible in an expository manner to feed the flock of God?

This last metaphor of a farmer also emphasizes the importance of patience. Farmers have to be some of the most patient people on earth. We read in James 5:7–8: "Be patient, therefore, brothers, until the coming of the Lord. See how the farmer waits for the precious fruit of the earth, being patient about it, until it receives the early and the late rains. You also, be patient. Establish your hearts, for the coming of the Lord is at hand."

Paul closes this passage by telling Timothy, "Think over what I say." This is not just casual musing. Paul means for Timothy to ponder, meditate, and pray about the things of God. You will never clearly hear the voice of God unless you spend time listening to Him. You must spend time in prayer, both talking and listening to Him and spend time daily in His Word.

Paul's overall charge to his young protégé is this: "Timothy, be faithful. In any and every circumstance, remain faithful to the gospel of the Lord Jesus Christ."

Hebrews 11:32–40 states:

> And what more shall I say? For time would fail me to tell of Gideon, Barak, Samson, Jephthah, of David and Samuel and the prophets—who through faith conquered kingdoms, enforced justice, obtained promises, stopped the mouths of lions, quenched the power of fire, escaped the edge of the sword, were made strong out of weakness, became mighty in war, put foreign armies to flight. Women received back their dead by resurrection. Some were tortured, refusing to accept release, so that they might rise again to a

better life. Others suffered mocking and flogging, and even chains and imprisonment. They were stoned, they were sawn in two, they were killed with the sword. They went about in skins of sheep and goats, destitute, afflicted, mistreated—of whom the world was not worthy—wandering about in deserts and mountains, and in dens and caves of the earth.

And all these, though commended through their faith, did not receive what was promised, since God had provided something better for us, that apart from us they should not be made perfect.

How were these men and women able to remain faithful through all of these trials and tribulations? Here's the answer in the first two verses of the next chapter of Hebrews: "Therefore, since we are surrounded by so great a cloud of witnesses, let us also lay aside every weight, and sin which clings so closely, and let us run with endurance the race that is set before us, looking to Jesus, the founder and perfecter of our faith, who for the joy that was set before him endured the cross, despising the shame, and is seated at the right hand of the throne of God."

Do you want to know how to stand strong in the face of suffering? Look to Jesus. I think all of our problems in the church today can be traced back to our looking away from Jesus and getting off course. If we stay focused on the Lord Jesus Christ, we will be able to stand strong in any circumstance.

If Paul had been in the Marine Corps, I think he would have repeated the marines' slogan to Timothy. If you're a marine, you would tell me, "It's not just a slogan; it's a way of life." The slogan is the two-word phrase *Semper Fidelis*. Sometimes you see it abbreviated *Semper Fi*. *Semper Fidelis* means "always faithful." I think that's what Paul would tell Timothy: "Semper Fi, my brother. Always faithful. Don't ever give up. No matter what happens, remain faithful to the Lord Jesus Christ." And that's what I want to challenge you with today. Don't ever give up.

When Dr. Jim Richards spoke at the Southern Baptist Texas Convention, he gave a powerful charge as a part of his speech, and I want to share it with you. He said:

I am a soldier. Here I stand. I am a soldier, a prayer warrior of the army of my God. The Lord Jesus Christ is my Commanding Officer. The Holy Bible is my code of conduct. Faith, prayer, and the Word of God are my weapons of warfare. I have been taught by the Holy Spirit, trained by experience, tried in adversity, tested by fire.

I am a volunteer in the army of God, and I am enlisted for eternity. I will either retire at the rapture or die in His army; but I will not get out, sell out, or be talked out. I am faithful, capable, and dependable. If my God needs me, I am there.

I am a soldier in the army of God. I am a prayer warrior. Here I stand. I'm not a baby. I do not need to be pampered or petted; don't need to be primed up, or pumped up, or picked up, or pepped up. No one has to call me, or write me, or visit me, or entice me, or lure me. I am not a wimp. I am in place, saluting my King, obeying His orders, praising His name, and building His Kingdom.

I am a soldier. I am a prayer warrior, and here I stand. No one has to send me flowers, gifts, food, cards, candy, or give me hand-outs. I do not need to be cuddled or cared for or catered to.

I am committed. I cannot have my feelings hurt badly enough to turn me around. I cannot be discouraged enough to turn me aside. I cannot lose enough to make me quit. When Jesus called me into the army, I had nothing. If I end up with nothing, I will still come out even.

I will win. My God will supply all my needs. I am more than a conqueror. I will always triumph. I can do all things through Christ Jesus, because I am a soldier, a prayer warrior, and here I stand. Devils cannot defeat me. People cannot disillusion me. Weather cannot beat me. Sickness cannot stop me. Battles cannot beat me. Money cannot buy me. Governments cannot silence me and hell cannot handle me.

Here I stand. I'm a soldier, a prayer warrior. Even death cannot destroy me. For when my Commander calls me from this battlefield, He will promote me to a captain and He will bring me back to this world to rule with Him.

I am a soldier, a prayer warrior, in the army of God, and I'm marching. I'm claiming victory. I will not give up. I will not turn around. I am a soldier, a prayer warrior, and marching heaven-bound. Here I stand! Will you stand with me[11]?

That's powerful. Can you say that? You might find yourself saying, "I want to be a part of that team." In order to be enlisted into the Army of God, you've got to know the Commander in Chief personally. His name is Jesus. The way to establish a personal relationship with God is by repenting of your sins and accepting the sacrifice that Jesus made on the cross to save you from your sins.

As you grow in your walk with the Lord, pursue opportunities to be discipled by more mature believers in the faith. And look for opportunities to disciple others like Paul discipled his spiritual son in the faith, Timothy. That's the only way to leave a spiritual legacy with lasting impact.

chapter 7

Staying Faithful, No Matter What

2 TIMOTHY 2:8-10

All through the book of 2 Timothy, Paul is preparing Timothy to expect suffering and hardship as he preaches the gospel. I'm sure that Timothy is starting to wonder, "But *how* am I going to endure this kind of suffering? How can I keep the faith, no matter what?" That's the question I want to answer in this chapter.

In 2 Timothy 2:8–10, Paul writes,

> 8 Remember Jesus Christ, risen from the dead, the offspring of David, as preached in my gospel, 9 for which I am suffering, bound with chains as a criminal. But the word of God is not bound! 10 Therefore I endure everything for the sake of the elect, that they also may obtain the salvation that is in Christ Jesus with eternal glory.

Paul starts with the word *remember.* In the Greek, this word is interesting because it's in the present active tense, which tells us that this is something Paul is calling Timothy to do every single day. "Remember constantly," he is saying. "Timothy, continually remember these things."

Remember the Gospel You Have Heard

Paul reminds Timothy to first *remember the gospel you have heard.* He wants his young friend to know that when the going gets tough in ministry, this is where he should turn. He says, "Remember Jesus Christ, risen from the dead, the offspring of David, as preached in my gospel."

Paul wants Timothy to remember the life of Jesus, the death of Jesus, and the resurrection of Jesus. He wants Timothy to keep in mind that *God demonstrated His authority through Jesus' resurrection.* That's why he says, "Remember Jesus Christ, risen from the dead."

Before we talk further about Jesus' resurrection, let me tell you about His death. His death on the cross was anything but a bed of roses. At the end of His life—the portion of His life when He stood before the religious high priests and corrupt politicians—He suffered misery, He suffered desertion from His followers, He suffered pain and betrayal, He suffered persecution, and He was left all alone, hanging naked and bleeding on a Roman cross. Imagine what it was like for Jesus to endure that much suffering for our sin.

It is the realization of the difficulty and the hardship that Jesus went through when He chose to take on our sins and the sins of the entire world, even though He was sinless that makes the gospel Good News. He chose to endure that for us.

Thankfully, Jesus' death on the cross was not the end of the story. On the third day, He rose again from the dead. The resurrection is an intriguing doctrine. And not only that, it's absolutely central to our faith. A lot of us tend to just gloss over it because we've heard about it our entire lives, but Paul emphasizes its importance when he says, "Remember Jesus Christ, risen from the dead." Paul doesn't want Timothy to focus on Jesus' death as a past-tense event; he wants Timothy to focus on the fact that Jesus has been raised from the dead and that He is alive today!

We find 300 passages in the New Testament alone that deal with resurrection. Matthew 12:38–42 explains that the resurrection is a sign for unbelievers. In Luke chapter 24, the resurrection was the answer to believers' doubt. When believers doubted that Jesus had been raised from the dead, Jesus actually showed himself to Thomas (see John 20:24–28). Romans chapter 4 and 1 Corinthians chapter 15 say that the resurrection is the heart of the gospel. The resurrection addresses our fear of death and gives us hope for the future, according to John 11:25. And it is our hope for heaven, according to Philippians 3:20.

God actually raised His Son Jesus from the dead. Think about it. What if one of my church members were to call me and say, "My father just passed away and I was wondering if you would do the funeral in a few days, Pastor." Then about a week after the funeral, I get a phone call from the same man. "Pastor? Guess what? You know that funeral you did recently for my dad? Well, he's alive now. Walked right out of the grave. Can you believe it?" Pretty odd, right? It would make national news. Think about how amazing it truly was for God, through His power and authority, to raise Jesus from the dead and bring Him back to life again.

Paul emphasizes this for two reasons. The first is *to show God's eternal power*. The resurrection proves that God has both the authority and the ability to raise a man from the dead. Ephesians 1:19–21 says, "According to the working of his great might that he worked in Christ when he raised him from the dead and seated him at his right hand in the heavenly places, far above all rule and authority and power and dominion, and above every name that is named, not only in this age but also in the one to come."

Second, not only does God have eternal power, but *He grants us eternal life*. Jesus, being raised from the dead, gives us hope to know that we trust in a God who has conquered the grave, removed the shackles of sin, and set us free. Isn't that good news? The closer we get to death the greater that news will be, because we realize that we don't have to fear death anymore, right? We have hope in a God that has conquered death.

Paul writes in 1 Corinthians 15:54–56, "Death is swallowed up in victory. 'O death, where is your victory? O death, where is your sting?' The sting of death is sin, and the power of sin is the law. But thanks be to God, who gives us the victory through our Lord Jesus Christ." Death is defeated by Christ. We win in the end!

Paul tells Timothy that God exemplified His authority in the resurrection. And Paul also notes that God exemplified His authority through Jesus' role, as seen in the little phrase "the seed of David." Other Bible versions say "the offspring of David." Paul reminds Timothy that Jesus Christ, when He came into the world, fulfilled the prophecies of the Old Testament stating that He would descend through the lineage of King David. "The seed of David" is another term for the lineage of David. The fact that Jesus came through David's line is mentioned throughout the Bible. In the Old Testament, we see 300-plus scriptures predicting the coming of the Messiah. Then Jesus came and the New Testament reveals how He fulfilled every one of these prophecies.

One of the most convincing evidences we have to prove that Jesus is the Messiah is the fact that He fulfilled all of the prophecies about Him in the Old Testament. If anyone ever wants to try to convince you that Jesus was not the Messiah, just open up the Old Testament and show them how He fulfilled the prophecies of old. There are 17 prophecies of the Old Testament that speak of Jesus as being the Son of David. Paul is saying to Timothy, "God displayed His power by raising Jesus from the dead, but He also came through on His promise by bringing Jesus to earth through the lineage of David."

He says this to emphasize God's authority and our need to surrender our worry to Him. We serve a living and active God who has defeated the grave. John Stott writes, "Death is the gateway to life and suffering the path to glory. For he who died rose from the dead, and he who was born in lowliness as David's seed is now reigning in glory on David's throne."[12] I love that. Both expressions set forth in embryonic form the contrast between humiliation and exaltation.

We see the essence of humiliation in Jesus' death and burial, but the resurrection presents an exalted Jesus being raised from the dead and seated in royal splendor on the throne of David. That's why William and Gloria Gaither penned the words "Because he lives, I can face tomorrow." I believe that if Paul had been a hymn writer, he would have written that hymn.

Remember the Word You Were Taught

The second point we see in the text is that Paul wants Timothy to *remember the word that he was taught*. In verse 9, Paul tells us that although he is bound in chains for preaching the gospel, the Word of God cannot be bound.

Look at 1 Corinthians 2:1–2 to see this gospel message that Paul was preaching: "And I, when I came to you, brothers, did not come proclaiming to you the testimony of God with lofty speech or wisdom. For I decided to know nothing among you except Jesus Christ and him crucified."

This is certainly not the health, wealth, and prosperity gospel that we hear today. In fact, Paul would say that when you give your life to Jesus it's anything but an easy life. Paul would say, "Timothy, not only should you expect persecution, you should anticipate persecution because we're preaching about a man who came to live and die and was crucified for the very thing he believed in. And that's the thing I'm preaching."

Paul says that the Word of God is not bound. There were naysayers around, suggesting that if Paul was in prison then he was probably not an apostle! The joke was, "If Paul was really following God, he'd be out like we are. But we're free, and Paul is in jail." But Paul says, "They can talk badly about me all they want. They can try to hinder me from preaching the gospel. But the Word of God is living and active, and it will continue to go forth and bear fruit. It doesn't matter if I'm in prison or free; God's Word still stands."

I love that, because that's my job as a pastor. My job is to labor by God's grace over the Word of God, to listen to the voice of God, and to memorize and meditate on the Word of God so that on Sunday morning, I can give my congregation a word from God. And then it's the job of each individual to get into the Word until the Word gets into them personally. I can only feed my flock so much; Christians need to get to a place in their lives where they know how to feed themselves. That's the reason why I wrote the book *Creating an Atmosphere to Hear God Speak*. The book emphasizes the fact that when people get into the Word, they listen to God. And when you listen to God, you're more likely to be and to do what God wants.

You know, the Word of God is not confined to the printed page. The Word of God is not bound to typeset characters. It's not limited only to church services. It's alive and dynamic. Hebrews 4:12 says, "For the word of God is living and active, sharper than any two-edged sword, piercing to the division of soul and of spirit, of joints and of marrow, and discerning the thoughts and intentions of the heart." In Isaiah 55:11, God says, "So shall my word be that goes out from my mouth; it shall not return to me empty, but it shall accomplish that which I purpose, and shall succeed in the thing for which I sent it."

Of course, for centuries, people have tried to get rid of the Word of God. In AD 303, the Roman emperor Diocletian tried to eliminate the Word of God by issuing this decree: anyone preaching the Word would be persecuted and killed and all Bibles and writings about the Bible would be burned. Later, in 1536, Tyndale, the great Reformer, was persecuted for translating the Bible into English. He was a great translator, but not only did the religious leaders of the Catholic church want to persecute him, they also wanted to destroy his work. They wanted to burn not only everything written by Tyndale, but they also wanted to be burn Tyndale himself at the stake.

The Word of God is living and active, and men like Tyndale and the apostle Paul were willing to give their lives to defend it. That's why the great Reformer Martin Luther wrote these lines in the famous hymn "A Mighty Fortress Is Our God": "The body they may kill, God's truth abideth still."

Remember the Mission You've Been Given

In the third remembrance, Paul calls Timothy to *remember the mission he has been given.* He writes, "Therefore I endure everything for the sake of the elect, that they also may obtain the salvation that is in Christ Jesus with eternal glory." Paul means, "God has given me a mission, and the mission is to take the gospel to the nations." He's not talking about sharing God's Word with people who have already received the gospel, he's talking about preaching to those that God is about to call in the future. It's Paul's job to take the message to the nations.

Now, at this point some of us might get a little nervous because we see Paul using the term *elect.* Well, one of the reasons I love expository preaching and teaching is the fact that you can't get around words in the text. I have to preach the Word of God as it stands. Friends, let me share something with you. When we come to the word *elect*, we shouldn't get nervous. This is the Word of God, so we know that this term was chosen for a reason.

C. S. Lewis says that election and man's responsibility are like the doorway leading into a building. On one side above the doorway are painted the words "whosoever will come." When you walk through the doorway and look back, on the other side, you see the words "chosen before the foundation of the world." But it's the same door.

Let me share with you a couple of scriptures that will also help explain this relationship. Ephesians 1:4 says, "Even as he chose us in him before the foundation of the world, that we should be holy and blameless before him."

Romans 8:29 (NIV) says, "For those God foreknew he also predestined to be conformed to the likeness of his Son, that he might be the firstborn among many brothers."

Jesus says in John 6:65, "No one can come to me unless it is granted him by the Father."

God is a God of election. He chose Israel. Why didn't He choose the Egyptians? Why didn't He choose the Canaanites? Why didn't He choose the northern people? For reasons only He knows, He chose the Israelites to follow Him. That's just the way God is.

On the other hand we are given the choice to respond to Him. The ability to believe in God is a gift from Him. In Ephesians 2:8, Paul writes, "For by grace you have been saved through faith. And this is not your own doing; it is the gift of God . . . so that no one may boast." And in Matthew 11:28 Jesus says: "Come to me, all who labor and are heavy laden, and I will give you rest."

We find a connection in the text between God's choosing and Paul's going. But the primary emphasis in the text is not on the elect. The emphasis in the text is on the exclusivity of Jesus Christ. Paul is saying, "Yes, God has chosen people to follow Him. But it's your job to tell those people about Jesus." That's why Paul says in Romans 10:13–15: "For 'everyone who calls on the name of the Lord will be saved.' How then will they call on him in whom they have not believed? And how are they to believe in him of whom they have never heard? And how are they to hear without someone preaching? And how are they to preach unless they are sent? As it is written, 'How beautiful are the feet of those who preach the good news!'"

Here's the formula that Paul presents. When people are sent, they preach. When those people preach, other people hear. When people hear, they believe. And when they believe, they call on the name of the Lord. And when they call upon the name of the Lord, they will be saved. In order for people to be saved, we have to go. Whether you lean more toward the sovereignty of God or toward man's responsibility, here's the point: you and I are called to take the message of the Lord Jesus Christ to the nations. That's the mandate that God has ordained for our lives.

There's a serious problem in our culture. We stumble across that problem when we tell people the truth, which is that Jesus is the only way of salvation and the only way to the Father.

"Hmm," you might say. "Really? The *only* way? I'm not sure I like the exclusivity of that statement. You don't really believe that, do you?"

Yes, I absolutely believe that; not because of my own ideas, but because that's what the Bible says. Pure and simple.

Acts 4:12 says, "And there is salvation in no one else, for there is no other name under heaven given among men by which we must be saved." That name is Christ Jesus. In John 14:6, Jesus states plainly, "I am the way, the truth, and the life. No one comes to the Father except through me." Guess what *no one* means? Nobody. Not a single person. *No one* comes to the Father except through Christ Jesus. Paul was clearly willing to give up his very life for the belief that Jesus was not only the only way to heave, but would also raise him from the dead into eternal life.

Paul was motivated to serve Christ through difficult circumstances because of a spiritual truth that we can discover in the text. He reminds Timothy (and us) of the importance of focus. In Philippians 3:13–14, Paul writes, "One thing I do: forgetting what lies behind and straining forward to what lies ahead, I press on toward the goal for the prize of the upward call of God in Christ Jesus." He focuses on the task at hand.

In Philippians 3:7–8, Paul focuses on Christ "But whatever gain I had, I counted as loss for the sake of Christ. Indeed, I count everything as loss because of the surpassing worth of knowing Christ Jesus my Lord. For his sake I have suffered the loss of all things and count them as rubbish, in order that I may gain Christ."

In Philippians 4:8, Paul charges others to focus, "Finally, brothers, whatever is true, whatever is honorable, whatever is just, whatever is pure, whatever is lovely, whatever is commendable, if there is any excellence, if there is anything worthy of praise, think about these things. What you have learned and received and heard and seen in me—practice these things, and the God of peace will be with you."

Finally, In 2 Timothy 2:8, Paul focuses on the resurrected Christ, "Remember Jesus Christ, risen from the dead, the offspring of David, as preached in my gospel."

You may not be able to control your circumstances; you may have no control over your situation; you certainly can't control what other people do to you; but you can control what you focus on and how you respond. As Christians we have to focus on Christ, the gospel, the resurrection, and the Word of God that will endure forever. We must stay centered on the mission we've been given.

We see the importance of this truth when we realize the situation being faced by Timothy. He was seeing severe persecution of Christians all around him. He was starting to realize that the chance that he would die for the faith was high. He was seeing people beheaded left and right for following Christ. Paul's instruction to Timothy in these incredibly trying times was to maintain his focus on God.

Many of us are going through difficult times. Maybe you're going through financial issues or marital issues or family issues or have sons or daughters who have strayed from the Lord. You may not be able to control everything that happens to you, but you can definitely control what you focus on. Isn't it encouraging that before he dies Paul tells Timothy, "Here's the truth. By centering your life on Jesus, He'll get you through any situation."

That's why Hebrews 12:2 says this: "Looking to Jesus, the founder and perfecter of our faith, who for the joy that was set before him endured the cross, despising the shame, and is seated at the right hand of the throne of God."

I asked myself about focus as I was studying the Moravian missionaries. These men gave up their lives with selfless service to God through sacrificial living. They lived by and meditated on an inspiring motto that motivated them to go to the nations.

The story is told of two Moravian missionary boys who felt the call to go to the island of the West Indies. On this island lived an atheist British landowner who had two to three thousand slaves that he had brought in from all over the country to work on this island. He was so sick of religion that he said: "No preacher, no clergyman will ever stay on this island. If he becomes shipwrecked, we'll keep him in a separate house until he has to leave. But he's never going to talk to any of us about God. I'm through with all that nonsense."

Well, these two Moravian missionary boys heard about this British atheist landowner and decided to sell themselves into slavery to this man in order to reach him and others on that island for Christ. Can you imagine? They took the money they received from selling themselves into slavery and paid for a ship to take them to the island. This wasn't a four-year term; this was a lifetime commitment to Christ. These two boys actually sold themselves into a lifetime of slavery to reach that landowner and those two to three thousand other slaves.

You can imagine what their families thought as these two boys stood on the bow of the ship that day. "What is the wisdom in this? How could these two boys give up their lives for this?" These were two young men in their twenties. Imagine your sons or daughters at that age, leaving to sell themselves into slavery for a lifetime in order to win people to Christ. As the two boys stood on the bow of the boat, the other Moravian missionaries from Herrnhut came to see them off. With tears in their eyes, their family members watched.

As the gap widened between the ship and the shore, one Moravian boy locked his arm in the arm of the other Moravian missionary. He stood tall on the bow of the boat and yelled out the motto for why they went: "*May the Lamb that was slain receive the reward for His suffering!*" That was the motto of the Moravian missionary movement: that Jesus, the Lamb that was slain, would receive the reward for His suffering.

You know, when I heard that story, I tried to fathom what it would be like literally to give up my life to go into missions and to risk being killed. The risk was very real for these young men. The average lifespan in Africa was only two years for Moravian missionaries during that time. I asked myself, "When did those two missionary boys die?"

The answer is, "They died the moment that they decided to give their lives to Christ."

We know from his letters that Paul found to live is Christ, and to die is gain. He tells us he had been crucified with Christ, so that it was no longer himself living, but Christ in him. Paul did not die at the hands of the Romans, he died the day he met Jesus on the road to Damascus.

If you are not living with an attitude of selfless service to the Lord it is because you haven't died yet. In fact, you're very much alive to the things of the world and to yourself.

When I take a good, hard look at my own life, I wonder, "Robby, why are you not committed to the Lord the way you need to be?" I know that the reason is that I hang on to too many things of the world. Sometimes I focus too much on material things, things that I think will make me happy. Sometimes I get caught up in things that I feel will advance my ministry and my career success. That's what we all do, right? We start thinking that life is all about us. And that's why every day that I wake up, friends, I've got to die to self just like you do.

Jesus says it this way, "If anyone would come after me, let him deny himself and take up his cross and follow me" (Matthew 16:24).

Have you truly died to yourself?

chapter 8

Walking the Talk
of Selfless Living

2 TIMOTHY 2:11-13

Let's look again at 2 Timothy 2:8–13 to see how Paul helps Timothy understand the importance of dying to self in order to live for Christ:

> 8 Remember Jesus Christ, risen from the dead, the offspring of David, as preached in my gospel, 9 for which I am suffering, bound with chains as a criminal. But the word of God is not bound! 10 Therefore I endure everything for the sake of the elect, that they also may obtain the salvation that is in Christ Jesus with eternal glory. 11 The saying is trustworthy, for:
> If we have died with him, we will also live with him;
> 12 if we endure, we will also reign with him;
> if we deny him, he also will deny us;

13 if we are faithless, he remains faithful—
for he cannot deny himself.

In the previous chapter, I highlighted three things that Paul wants Timothy to remember:

- Remember the gospel you have heard.
- Remember the Word you have been taught.
- Remember the mission you've been entrusted with.

In this chapter, we'll look at the fourth element of the faith that Paul wants Timothy to remember, which is this: *remember the promise that you will obtain.* This promise relates to two aspects of Jesus' character: Jesus Christ, the Savior and Jesus Christ, the judge.

Jesus Christ, the Savior

We as believers will reside with Christ for eternity, and we as believers will also reign with Christ. My aim for this chapter is simple: I want to motivate you to stand strong in your faith and persevere to the end. That's my prayer for you.

In verse 11, Paul tells Timothy, "The saying is trustworthy." Paul uses this phrase only five times in the pastoral Epistles. First Timothy, 2 Timothy, and Titus are the pastoral Epistles. In addition, Paul uses this phrase *only* in the pastoral Epistles. You won't find it anywhere else in the New Testament.

When we see this phrase, the light bulb should come on and our antennae should go up because Paul means, "Come in close. Pay attention. Something important is about to be disclosed to you." In this passage, he leads into four lines that many commentators believe are drawn from an ancient hymn that was sung by new believers. Some believe that this hymn was sung before baptism: "If we have died with him, we will live; if we endure with him; we will reign."

When I was studying the connotation of this passage and got to the word *if*, I learned something interesting. In *Greek Grammar Beyond the Basics,* Professor Daniel Wallace tells us that in this context the reference to the gift is a first-class conditional statement. The *if* should not be translated as "if"; it should be translated as "since" (because). Paul is saying, "because we have died with him, we will also live. Because we endure, we will also reign."

The first challenge that Paul gives is that *we, as believers, will reside with Christ.* How exciting to know that we will live with Jesus Christ for all of eternity. In this passage, Paul is not just talking about death at the end of our earthly life; he's talking about a spiritual death. He's talking about the death that believers must enter into before we can be born again to life.

In order for you and me to live with Christ for eternity, we must experience a death of sorts. It's a spiritual death to sin and self. When you die to your sinful self, God raises you to new life in Christ. I'm sure we can agree that the text leads us to the idea of martyrdom at this point. You almost sense that Paul is thinking about the actual death of the body. We know that he is in prison as he writes this, fully aware that he is just a few days or moments away from his own death.

He seems to be saying, "Yes, Timothy, I'm going to die. And yes, you should be ready to die. But it's not only a physical death; you as a believer have to go through a spiritual death in order to identify with the Lord Jesus Christ." Jesus says it this way in Matthew 16:24, "If anyone would come after me, let him deny himself . . ." And do what? "Take up his cross [daily, which is death] and follow me."

Have you died to your former passions? Have you died to your former pleasures in the world? Because if you haven't, I would submit to you that you're not fully experiencing the spiritual life that you are meant to live. You can't be born again in Christ until you've died to your old habits and your old self, right?

Let me give you an interesting equation or a phrase to remember: if you're born once, you die twice. But if you're born twice, you die once. What do I mean by that? Every person here on earth has been born once. We were physically born, which is how we entered the world. If you only experience this physical birth, you will die a physical death at the end of your earthly life, and then you will die a supernatural or a spiritual death when you stand before the Lord on the day of judgment.

On the other hand, if you are a believer in Christ, not only have you been born once, but you have been born again. You have been born twice! That means that you will die a physical death at the end of your life on earth, but you will have spiritual life. You will only experience one death; you will live for eternity with God.

So my question to you is, have you been born twice? This is something you want to get right. In order for you to live with Christ, you have to die with Christ. Right out of the gate, we have to understand that as believers we have to die in order to reside with Christ.

Now, here's some more good news: not only will we reside with Christ as believers, but *we will also reign with Christ*. I love this part. I did a study of the word *reign* that really brought it to life. The question is, how do we reign with Christ? The answer is we must endure. Paul says that if we endure, we will also reign with Him.

The Greek term *endure* is pregnant with meaning. It means "to hold your ground." Have you ever played a game of tug-of-war and tried to hold your ground? That's what this word means: to dig in your heels and hold your ground through suffering and difficulty. Paul is challenging Timothy, "Timothy, I am enduring this, and so I challenge you to endure this too. Why? Because if we endure, we will reign with Christ."

The word *reign* is where we get the word *kingdom*. It's from the same Greek root. Jesus talks about the kingdom of God all the time. He says, "Repent and believe the Good News of God for the kingdom of heaven is at hand." When you look at this word and translate it back into the original language, it also means if you endure, you will be a king together with Christ. Now, we know there is only One who is worthy to wear a crown, and that's Christ. But this phrase gives us the idea that this is not a fictitious promise in the future. Paul is saying that this will be a reality for all the believers in Christ who endure to the end. He promises that your eternal reward will transcend eternal rest and lead to eternal responsibility.

Did you realize that God is going to give us responsibility in heaven? Scripture states that we will receive rewards in heaven. You and I will be rewarded with a level of authority in heaven. These rewards are given according to our service on earth. Yes, you're saved by grace through faith in Christ, but God determines what you will do in heaven based on what you do on earth.

I have two scriptures to prove this point. In Matthew chapter 25, Jesus tells the story of the talents. The master leaves on a trip and says, "I'm going to give five talents to my servant, I'm going to give two talents to this servant, and I'll give one talent to this servant." He comes back and the servant with five talents had turned it into ten. The master says, "Well done, my good and faithful servant." The man with two turned it into four and the master says, "Well done, my good and faithful servant." But the servant with one talent buried it and did not earn any return on his master's investment. The master says, "You wicked and slothful servant. Be removed from my presence. Be cast out into the outer darkness."

In First Corinthians 6:2 Paul says, "Do you not know that the saints will judge the world?" We are the saints in this verse. If you don't believe me, look at the beginning of most of Paul's letters. There are addressed to saints: to the saints in Rome who are loved by God and called to be saints, to all who are in Corinth, to the saints of Philippi. The saints are believers in Christ.

Did you know that, as believers, we will even judge angels? That's what Paul writes in 1 Corinthians 6:3: "Do you not know that we are to judge angels?" As believers in Jesus Christ, as a reward for our endurance, you and I will be able to judge angels. Now, I don't know about you, but

I'm not real excited about judging angels when I've got enough issues of my own.

You and I will be rewarded for our endurance. Our endurance in the faith does not *earn* our salvation, but our endurance to the end *proves* our salvation. You can't be more saved today than you were yesterday. You can't do anything more to earn merit from God. Your faithfulness to the end will prove your faith in God. The actions of your life will prove to God and to the world that you are a believer in Jesus Christ.

Why does Paul remind Timothy of this? Have you thought about that? I think Paul is teaching us all a valuable lesson: Whatever you focus on you is what you will achieve. Paul wants Timothy to focus on the end goal. He's saying, "Focus on the fact that as bad as it gets and as difficult as life is you will live for eternity because you have died with Christ, and you will reign as a king with Jesus because you have endured." That's quite an incredible promise. The Christian life is a life of dying and enduring. The only way to live is to die. The only way to glory is through suffering.

Jesus Christ, the Judge

Next, Paul makes a shift in the context and begins to focus on Christ as the judge in verses 12 and 13. The important point he makes is that *Christ's response to us will be reciprocal.* What does that mean? It means that however you respond to Christ, He will respond to you. It's pretty simple.

The word *deny* in the language of the New Testament means "to disown" or "to refuse." It's used thirty-three times in the New Testament, and three of those instances appear in these two verses. Paul is saying in essence, "If you (future tense) ever deny Christ, Christ will (future tense) deny you." It's not just a present denial. Any time you deny Christ in the future, He will deny you. This reminds us of Jesus' words in Matthew 10:32–33: "So everyone who acknowledges me before men, I also will acknowledge before my Father who is in heaven, but whoever denies me before men, I also will deny before my Father who is in heaven."

In 2 Timothy 1:15, Paul mentions two men named Hermogenes and Phygelus. These two men turned their backs on Paul. Paul knows what it's like to be denied and betrayed. These two men did not turn their backs on Christ; however, they simply turned their backs on Paul.

In contrast, the men Paul mentions in 2 Timothy 2:17, Hymenaeus and Philetus, actually turned their back on Christ. Paul writes in verse 18, they "have swerved from the truth, saying that the resurrection has already happened. They are upsetting the faith of some." Here, we find the idea of someone following Christ but then turning his back on Him.

The word *swerve* actually means "to miss the mark." It means "to set out on a path aimed in the wrong direction." It appears that these men set out to follow Christ, but they turned aside. Maybe they were following Him for the wrong reasons. Don't we know people like that? They say they follow Christ, but in their hearts they are following for all the wrong reasons. That kind of follower will swerve from the truth.

If a person in the future denies Christ openly, that means that he or she never possessed Christ personally. If you are a believer, you may deny Christ from time to time (like the apostle Peter did), but you will not stay in that denial. Your life will be the proof to God and to the world that you are a true believer in Christ. Your actions will prove your faith.

In 2 Timothy 3:1–5, Paul warns Timothy about certain individuals: "But understand this: that in the last days there will come times of difficulty. For people will be lovers of self, lovers of money, proud, arrogant, abusive, disobedient to their parents, ungrateful, unholy, heartless, unappeasable, slanderous, without self-control, brutal, not loving good, treacherous, reckless, swollen with conceit, lovers of pleasure rather than lovers of God, having the appearance of godliness, but denying its power. Avoid such people." Paul means that many people in our churches may appear godly, but secretly are not. We should do all we can to avoid these people.

Conversely, church history is full of examples of people who courageously gave their lives for the faith and refused to deny Christ, no matter what. Marcus Aurelius is one example. He was commanded by Julian the Apostate to give money to a heathen temple, but he refused.

As a result, Julian's men held Marcus Aurelius down and began to cut him with knives and lancets all over his body. They said, "If you agree to give just half a penny to the temple, we'll let you go. If you agree to burn incense to an idol in the temple, we'll let you go." But he didn't. After he had been cut wide open, they poured honey all over his body, put him in a room and let bees and wasps sting him to death.

Until his dying breath, Marcus Aurelius said, "I'd rather die than disown Christ."

Now, you may be saying, "Me too, Pastor. I would never deny Christ. I would never do that." But we do not only deny Christ with our words. Do you ever deny Christ with your actions? Do you ever deny Him with your attitudes? How often do you deny Him by looking at things you shouldn't? How about the places you go?

I believe that if we really stop and take a good, hard look at our lives, all of us would be guilty of sin in this area. We may not deny Christ openly, but we deny Him in our hearts. We deny Him in our lives.

I hear this all the time on Sunday, especially when I'm leaving church. People come up to me and say, "Please pray for my family member. He's struggling with (blank)."

Often, I ask them, "Has he ever surrendered his life to the Lord Jesus Christ and given Him his life completely?"

Their response is always, "Yes. Twenty years ago, he made a decision in this very church. He walked down the aisle and signed a card."

My next question is this: "Does he live a life of holiness?"

"No."

"Does he have a heart for the Lord?"

"No."

"Does he read his Bible?"

"No."

"Does he pray?"

"No."

"Does he come to church on Sunday morning or Wednesday night or Sunday night?"

"No, he never comes to church. We hardly ever see him. He has a filthy mouth. He's always telling dirty jokes. He's always going to places he shouldn't go to. He's at the bar on Friday night. He's out with his friends on Saturday night. You ought to hear the way he talks to his wife and treats his kids. But we're still holding onto the fact that twenty years ago he accepted Christ."

Friends, your life will prove (or disprove) your faith. Don't take my word for it; take the Lord's Word for it. If you deny Christ in attitude or motive or deed or action or thought, you are denying Him. And if you do that, the Bible says that He will deny you. Don't you think that when you come in contact with the living God, your life should manifest visible signs of your relationship and your engagement with Him? Don't you think there should be signs in your life that you met God and were transformed? Your life and your actions will prove (or disprove) your faith.

Finally, Paul says, *Christ's response to you will be faithful.* Adrian Rogers has a great quote about this: "A faith that fizzles before the finish had a flaw from the first." It means that if a person's faith fizzles out, it's probably because he or she never had a firm foundation in Christ in the first place. I call these people bottle-rocket Christians. They go up with a bang—but then they burn out. Let's not be those with a fizzling faith.

Now, notice the last part of this text. It can be a little confusing. In fact, I spent quite a bit of time studying and wrestling with this part of the text. In 2 Timothy 2:13, Paul says in paraphrase, "Even if we are faithless to God, He remains faithful to us." This part of the text takes a different turn from the preceding verse. The previous part was a negative judgment; this is a promise. The promise is that even when you are faithless, God will be faithful.

The word *faithless* means "to act in a disloyal manner," "to act without faith," or "to prove false." It doesn't mean that you have lost your faith or are struggling with your faith; it's the idea that you never possessed saving faith at all. You've never possessed the faith that is able to save you. Many commentators have accurately argued that even when we are faithless, God remains faithful. Paul writes in 2 Timothy 1:12, "For I know whom I have believed, and I am convinced that he is able to guard until that Day what has been entrusted to me."

Hebrews 10:23 says, "Let us hold fast to the confession of our hope without wavering, for he who promised is faithful." We know that God remains faithful to us both when we are faithful and when we are faithless.

But in order for us to fully understand these verses, we have to understand the context of the passage. Verses 11 through 13 make up an epigram, which is a series of two parallel expressions to prove one point.

Here's the first part: if we die and endure, we live and we reign. Here's the second part: if we deny and we are faithless, He denies us and He is faithful to His Word—"If you deny Me, I will deny you."

Here are two different scenarios. Person A is described in the first two verses: he has a salvation experience with the Lord Jesus Christ. He hears the gospel. He believes. He repents of his sin and trusts in Christ through repentance. At the end of his life, he endures, and he goes on to be with Christ in heaven.

Person B hears the gospel but he rejects it. Because of his rejection, he lives a life of serving only himself. He lives in sin. At the end of his life, he denies Christ and is faithless, and because of that, he goes to hell. The renowned preacher Charles Spurgeon spoke about this passage, discussing those who, like Person B, choose to deny Christ with their life and their actions. Consider what he says,

> They will say, 'Lord, we once took the Lord's Supper. Lord, we were once members of the church. But there came a time when times became hard for us. My mother caused me to give up religion. My father was angry with You. The trade in our business went bad. I was mocked all the time. I could not stand it. Lord, I fell among the evil acquaintances and they tempted me to turn. I could not resist it. I was Your servant. I did love You. I've always loved You in my heart; but I could not help it, God. I denied you. I went to the world again.'

What will Jesus say to that man on the Day of Judgment?

He will say, "I do not know you. Where are you?"

"But Lord, I want You to be my Advocate."

"I do not know you. Where are you?"

"But Lord, I cannot get into heaven unless you open the gates for me."

"I do not know you. I know you not."

"But Lord, my name is in the church book."

"I do not know you. I deny you."

"But Lord, do you not hear my cries, Lord?"

"You did not hear my cries," He will say. "You denied me, and therefore I deny thee."

"Lord, at least give me the lowest place in heaven so that I can escape the wrath to come."

"No, you will not look at the lowest place on earth and will not enjoy the lowest place here. You have made your choice, and you chose evil. You chose to be filthy; therefore be filthy. You chose to be unholy; therefore be unholy. I do not know you."[13]

Now, here's the good thing about this message. Spurgeon is not talking about believers; he's talking about unbelievers. At the end of our lives, not only will God be faithful to His Word but also He will be faithful to *your* word.

Some people say to God all their lives, "God, leave me alone! I want nothing to do with you." At the end of their lives, guess what God will say? "Fine. You have your wish!" If you deny Him, He will deny you. And if you are faithless, He remains faithful to His Word because He cannot go against His Word.

The question is simple: are you living for Christ, or are you denying Christ? I know that there have been times in my life when I've acted a certain way and "talked the talk," but I didn't walk the walk. I lived another way. So I want to ask you right now to examine the landscape of your life. Are you being faithful to the Lord, or are you denying Him? Are you living in a way that is truthful, or are you living a lie?

chapter 9

Treating God's Word with the Attention It Deserves

2 TIMOTHY 2:14-19

I want to ask you an unusual question: are you a Berean or a babbler? According to Acts chapter 17, the apostle Paul left Thessalonica to travel to Berea. He noticed something special and different about the Christians there. He writes in Acts 17:10–12: "The brothers immediately sent Paul and Silas away by night to Berea, and when they arrived they went into the Jewish synagogue. Now these Jews were more noble than those in Thessalonica; they received the word with all eagerness, examining the Scriptures daily to see if these things were so. Many of them therefore believed, with not a few Greek women of high standing as well as men."

These Christian men and women didn't just blindly accept Paul's teaching as truth; they examined it carefully according to the rest of

God's Word. That's what I want to challenge you to do also. Using scripture as our guide, I want to give you three steps for developing an educated method for biblical examination in order to keep you from being misled by false teaching.

Let's take a look at 2 Timothy 2:14–19:

> 14 Remind them of these things, and charge them before God not to quarrel about words, which does no good, but only ruins the hearers. 15 Do your best to present yourself to God as one approved, a worker who has no need to be ashamed, rightly handling the word of truth. 16 But avoid irreverent babble, for it will lead people into more and more ungodliness, 17 and their talk will spread like gangrene. Among them are Hymenaeus and Philetus, 18 who have swerved from the truth, saying that the resurrection has already happened. They are upsetting the faith of some. 19 But God's firm foundation stands, bearing this seal: "The Lord knows those who are his," and, "Let everyone who names the name of the Lord depart from iniquity."

Be a Diligent Student of the Word

Paul offers Timothy three important challenges in this passage. The first challenge is this: *be a diligent student of the Word.* In order to be a diligent student of the Word, Paul says that we need to *eliminate word fights.* He writes, "Remind them of these things, and charge them before God not to quarrel about words." It's interesting that Paul puts a double emphasis at the beginning of this text. He says, "Timothy, remind them and charge them." In Greek, the phrase translated *quarrel about words* means "to get into a word fight" or "to debate the meanings of words." Don't let divisive attitudes get in the way of fellowship among the body.

The commentary by J. N. D. Kelly tells us: "Theological discussions which are purely verbal have nothing to do with the realities of the Christian faith."[14] Paul warned Timothy about these arguments on a number of occasions. We find one example in 1 Timothy 6:3–4 where Paul addresses the problem of people who are causing division in the body. He writes,

"If anyone teaches a different doctrine and does not agree with the sound words of our Lord Jesus Christ and the teaching that accords with godliness, he is puffed up with conceit and understands nothing. He has an unhealthy craving for controversy and for quarrels about words which produce envy, dissension, slander, evil suspicions. . . ." Paul wants Timothy to know that God will avenge those who cause division in the church with word fights.

Eliminating these word fights from our churches may be more difficult than just identifying them and certainly requires more work. In order to follow this instruction, we need to obey Paul's second charge: *immerse yourself in the Word*. Paul says, "Do your best to present yourself to God as one approved, a worker who has no need to be ashamed, rightly handling the Word of truth." *Do your best* means to be diligent. It means to work hard, to labor, and to persevere in your quest to learn and share the Word.

I like the fact that Paul is sure to tell Timothy to present himself to God as one approved. Notice that he didn't say, "Present yourself to other Christians" or "present yourself to the church leaders" or "present yourself to your congregation." What a relief to know that whether you are a Sunday School teacher, leader, deacon, or anyone who is serving the Lord, you only have to worry about pleasing God. When Paul says, "Present yourself to God," the word *present* means "to come alongside someone." It's the idea of showing yourself approved to the Lord, to be justified in His eyes.

You can be assured that when you present yourself to God, He will be examining your life to find out if you are handling His Word correctly. This isn't just for pastors or church leaders, but for every Christian. Are you handling God's Word correctly? Are you sharing the gospel with other people in a compelling way? Are you rightly dividing the Word of truth?

The word *dividing* can be traced back to the Greek root *orthos*. It's where we get English words like "orthodoxy" and "orthopedic." This word carries the idea of someone cutting or dividing something in a straight line. For instance, it's the image of a farmer plowing a field in a straight line in order to plant crops, a seamstress taking scissors and cutting a straight line in the fabric, or a stone mason laying bricks in a straight line to build a house.

Paul's career was devoted to preaching the gospel, but he made money to support his missionary efforts by making tents. If anybody knew what it was like to cut a straight line in the material of a tent, it was Paul. He wants to convey to Timothy the importance of accurately and meticulously dividing the Word of Truth.

One of the most effective ways to understand Scripture is through an inductive method of study. Similarly, the most effectual method for communicating Scripture is through expository preaching. Just because a pastor preaches from the Bible doesn't mean he is rightly dividing and accurately teaching the Word of God. It follows that church members should be studying under a pastor who is using the appropriate teaching methods to proclaim the Word.

In his book *Speaking God's Word*, Peter Adams describes some of the types of sermons that we hear from the pulpit today. I want to share just a few of them. The first sermon is the *proof text sermon*. Someone preaching a proof text sermon takes a text of scripture, reads it to the church at the beginning of the service, and never returns to the text again. You've heard this before. It's as if the pastor runs off the diving board of the text, jumps into the water, and never returns to the text again. The proof text sermon is used to prove what the pastor wants to say.

Peter Adams attended a Christmas Eve service where the pastor preached on Revelation 11:10. This is the text: "and those who dwell on the earth will rejoice over them and make merry and exchange presents." The pastor's point was that Christmas is a time for people to be joyful and send gifts to one another. He concluded his sermon by saying, "Have a Merry Christmas." Unfortunately, the second part of that verse says, "because these two prophets had been a torment to those who dwell on the earth." The reason people were rejoicing in the text is that two of God's servants had died. The pastor completely missed what the text (and the context) really said. Unfortunately this is common in a *proof text sermon.*

The second type of sermon is the *felt need sermon.* This type of sermon is viewed through the eyes of the psychological world. It's the therapeutic or moralistic sermon. It tends to focus on social or domestic issues. No matter what happens, the preacher always comes back to this idea of how to have greater success in your life, or how to focus on the family, the flag, or the fact that you need to give more money to the church. You've heard these before. These sermons are based on the idea that the preacher's job is to make you feel happy or healthy or to "have your best life now."

A final type of sermon is the *moralizing sermon.* This is the type of sermon in which the preacher moralizes the text. An example of this would be Philippians 3:13–14: "But one thing I do: forgetting what lies behind and straining forward to what lies ahead, I press on toward the goal. . . ." Then the preacher preaches for the next forty minutes about how Paul said you need to focus on setting and reaching your personal goals in life. The problem is, when you read the rest of verse 14, you discover that Paul's goal was to pursue "the prize of the upward call of God in Christ Jesus." Paul was certainly focused; but he was focused on Jesus Christ, not earthly goals.

The *expository preaching* method directly opposes these first three types of sermons. In an expository sermon, a pastor takes the text, studies it, and prays over it. Then he consults other resources (like Bible dictionaries, concordances, commentaries, and so on) to help him discover, as accurately as possible, the thought, context, and intent of the text before he preaches it to the people. As a man of God, the greatest gift that I can give to my church members is the gift of showing myself approved as I learn, labor, preach, and teach what God has said in His Word. My congregation doesn't just want to hear from me every Sunday morning; they want me to stand up and tell them, "Thus says the Lord." The only way I can do that is through expository preaching.

R. Kent Hughes says, "Sadly, what Paul tells Timothy flies directly in the face of so much preaching today, where instead of faithful exposition, there is disexposition. The text is announced and read and is so rich and promising and the people settle back in their pews, Bibles opened for a good Sunday meal, only to find that the text has departed, never to return."[15] Disexposition, Hughes says, leads to "Sunday indigestion."

Martin Luther said there were some in his day that were so nice and precise about the letter of scripture that they began to deliver an exposition on the book of Job. By the time they got to the tenth chapter of Job, these men had plagued the exposition of the text so much that Job suffered more losses from the expositors than from the trials that happened in his own life.

This is remarkably similar to what is happening in the world today. But Paul is calling us to communicate the Word of God accurately and appropriately. And this takes work. It's not easy to preach expository messages. You may be saying, "Well, I've heard plenty of expository sermons that were boring." How can the Word, which is living, active, and sharper than any two-edged sword, piercing even to the division of soul and spear and joint and marrow, discerning the thoughts and the intentions of the heart, be made boring? When the Word of God is communicated in a boring manner, it is detrimental to the entire congregation.

Disassociate with False Teachers

Not only does Paul instruct us to be diligent students of the Word; he also teaches that we need to *disassociate yourselves from false teachers*. In verse 16, Paul says that there are men in the congregation, among whom "are Hymenaeus and Philetus," who are spreading "irreverent babble" that will lead to "more and more ungodliness."

Isn't it amazing that he calls these guys out by name in his letter to the church? Paul doesn't just say, "Two men are causing division." He names the names of the two men who are responsible. God has called you and me as ministers of the gospel to live lives of holiness and obedience to God. These men proved by their actions that they were not living this way.

The first step you and I need to take when someone is teaching a false doctrine is to *analyze their talk*. These two men were spreading irreverent babble. That phrase *irreverent babble* can be translated as "godless chatter" or "empty words." It's amazing that in every one of the pastoral Epistles, Paul deals with this issue.

In 1 Timothy 6:20, Paul says, "O Timothy, guard the deposit entrusted to you. Avoid the irreverent babble and contradictions of what is falsely called 'knowledge,' for by professing it some have swerved from the faith."

The Complete Word Study Dictionary New Testament defines "irreverent babble" (Greek, *kenophonia*) as "senseless or wicked discourses, speeches that are devoid of any divine or spiritual character."[16]

When it comes to false teachers, you must first analyze their talk. Second, you need to *analyze their teaching*. These men were saying that the resurrection had already happened. This is significant because these two men were teaching that the second coming of Christ (the second resurrection, in which all believers in Christ will be raised in bodily form to be with Christ and to come back and reign on earth) had already taken place.

The second coming of Christ is so closely linked to Jesus' first resurrection from the dead that, in essence, these men were teaching that because we had not been raised a second time, Jesus has not be raised the first time. Paul calls them out because their destructive theologies were creating heresy within the church.

Paul says in 1 Corinthians 15:12–14: "Now if Christ is proclaimed as raised from the dead, how can some of you say that there is no resurrection of the dead? But if there is no resurrection of the dead, then not even Christ has been raised. And if Christ has not been raised, then our preaching is in vain and your faith is in vain."

If Jesus Christ has not been raised from the dead, then every Sunday you and I are wasting our time at church, right? That means we have nothing to look forward to. But we know that Jesus Christ *was* raised from the dead. So Paul instructs Timothy to look these two men in the eye and tell them they're causing division.

Do you remember what Jesus would do when He encountered people possessed by demons? The demons knew who Jesus was, and they would try to speak out to Him, saying things like, "Leave us alone" or "Jesus, you are the Son of David." Jesus would always silence them. I think that the reason Jesus silenced the demons is because a holy message cannot be carried in an unholy vessel. You can't preach a holy gospel and be unholy to the Lord.

False teachers, through their actions, will show you that they're false. Their teaching will impact the church in three ways. First, *it will lead people to ungodliness*. If you associate with false teachers, they will lead you to be ungodly. In the text, the idea is that these men were preaching perverted truth. Keep in mind that Paul is not just talking to unbelievers or immature believers; he's talking to Timothy. Even as a seasoned Christian disciple of the apostle Paul, Timothy was warned to be wary of deception and becoming caught up in the irreverent babble of these men. Friends, heresy and false teaching can disguise themselves at any time and try to rise up and lead us into ungodliness. That's why we need to be aware of this.

John MacArthur says this about pastors and false teachers:

> No one is ever exempt from the corruptive influence of falsehood in the church. Just as a doctor cannot help from being exposed to dangerous diseases that he is treating, the godly preacher or teacher cannot help from being exposed to dangerous ideas in the church. But just as the doctor keeps exposure to a minimum and concentrates on destroying the disease, the godly preacher and teacher must expose the falsehood and then treat it correctly and exterminate it with truth.[17]

False teaching leads to ungodliness, and second, *it spreads like gangrene*. What a vivid picture of the reality of false teaching. The word *gangrene* is the Greek word *gaggraina*. It's a disease that rapidly spreads throughout the body. If not treated immediately, it will destroy its victim. The word *spreads* is the Greek word for *pasture*. If pastors aren't careful, this cancerous disease will spread like a large flock of sheep scattering out in an open field.

If you get gangrene in your arm and it's not treated immediately, it will spread to your other body parts. If you don't treat it, the affected body parts will have to be amputated. Eventually the gangrene will enter your bloodstream and travel to your heart. This disease will ultimately kill you. Friends, if false teaching and division within a church are not addressed immediately, parts of the body will be severed and that church will be divided and possibly destroyed altogether. Have you ever noticed when God moves the enemy always has a counter move in the church? It's like a game of chess. I'm sure that Paul was seeing many people come to know the Lord, and so the devil was trying to attack the church.

Third, *false teaching will ruin the faith of others.* This word *ruin* is the word for *catastrophe*. It describes a catastrophic destruction that comes upon a church or an individual. If a pastor does not identify and address false teaching in the church, he will find himself with a catastrophic problem on his hands. The only way to identify and address false teachers within the church is with the Word of God. Are you a vessel of blessing, or are you a vessel of babble? Are you a vessel of honor to the Lord, or are you a vessel of discord? Paul charges Timothy's church as well as the church of today to consider these questions.

This charge also comes with a promise from God. At first, I thought verse 19 was part of the next section, but the more I studied it, I realized that this is actually the exclamation point of the entire passage. Paul is quoting from Numbers chapter 16, a passage that describes several men who rose up against Moses.

Here's a good hermeneutical, or interpretative, principle for you to remember. When you see a New Testament passage that quotes an Old Testament scripture, you need to go back to that scripture so you can understand the context and the principle being taught. That will give you insight into the meaning of the New Testament passage. Paul is using this reference to encourage Timothy to study this Old Testament passage in relation to the problems being faced by his church.

The Numbers passage describes Korah, Dathan, and Abiram and some 250 other leaders in the church who rose up against Moses. They confronted Moses and Aaron and refused to submit to their pastoral authority.

Numbers 16:3 says, "They assembled themselves together against Moses and against Aaron and said to them, 'You have gone too far! For all in the congregation are holy, every one of them, and the LORD is among them. Why then do you exalt yourselves above the assembly of the LORD?' "

Immediately, Moses fell on his face before the Lord. This makes a powerful statement to pastors and church leaders. If someone attacks us, before we retaliate or take action, we must pray. That's what Moses did. He fell prostrate before the Lord. Then, after he stood up, he said to Korah and company in verse 5: "In the morning the LORD will show who is his, and who is holy, and will bring him near to him. The one whom he chooses he will bring near to him."

The Lord knows who are His; there's the connection with Timothy's situation. We see this in the way the story plays out. Korah and his men gathered with 250 other Israelites; Moses and Aaron stood opposite of them. Suddenly, the earth opened up, and Korah, Dathan, Abiram, and all the others who opposed Moses were sucked down into the earth. As if that were not enough, God sent a "firebomb" from heaven that came down and incinerated the dissenters right in front of all the people watching. Then Moses said in verse 34: "And all Israel who were around them fled at their cry out, for they said, 'Lest the earth swallow us up!'" God delivered Moses from the rebels that day. He showed that the Lord knows who are His.

This should be a lesson to us not to grow disheartened by false teachers in the church (or outside of it) because God knows who is really on His side and who is not. God can tell the real thing from a fake. Paul told Timothy that God will judge and avenge in the end. When the decisive fires of judgment fall and this universe is just an afterthought, God will separate, once and for all, the sheep from the goats. He knows who is devoted to Him and who is not.

Depart from Iniquity

Finally, Paul charges Timothy (and us) to *depart from iniquity*. He reminds us that God is calling us to be holy. Paul refers back to Numbers 16:26 where Moses tells the Israelite people to separate themselves from Korah and the other disobedient men whom the Lord was about to destroy. Moses says, "Depart, please, from the tents of these wicked men, and touch nothing of theirs, lest you be swept away with all their sins." The Israelites were challenged not even to go near the tents of these wicked men.

Paul gives Timothy a similar command to refuse to have anything to do with a man or woman who is causing division in the church. He wants Timothy to remain committed to holiness, purity, and speaking God's truth. That's why he says in 1 Corinthians 6:19–20, "Do you not know that your body is a temple of the Holy Spirit within you, whom you have from God? You are not your own, for you were bought with a price. So glorify God in your body."

The apostle Peter also writes in 1 Peter 1:14–16, "As obedient children, do not be conformed to the passions of your former ignorance, but as he who called you is holy, you also be holy in all your conduct, since it is written, 'You shall be holy, for I am holy.' " God's challenge to us as His church is to abstain from immorality.

I want to emphasize something important in this text that you may have missed. Many of us just gloss over the names of Hymenaeus and Philetus, but I want to share with you something interesting about these two men. When Paul wrote a letter to any one of the churches, Paul knew that not only would the recipient read the letter, but that the person who received the letter would also stand up before the entire congregation and read it to the church. Paul knew that Hymenaeus and Philetus would be there in church that morning when Timothy got up and so bravely and eloquently read this letter. I'm sure that their wives and children were there as well.

Hymenaeus and Philetus had disguised themselves as "good church members." They might have been the first-century equivalent of leaders or deacons in the church. Outwardly, they appeared to be believers, but actually they were false teachers. Imagine if Paul had written this letter to your church, and your name was in it. What if he had said, "Avoid irreverent babble, for it will lead to more and more ungodliness and it will spread like gangrene, among whom are David and Michael or (insert your name here). Have nothing to do with those two." What a challenge to us!

But the good news is that God has not left us to learn this on our own. He has given us His Word. When we immerse ourselves in the Word of God by studying it and memorizing it, we learn to identify false teachers and separate them from real, godly teachers. And even more important, we draw closer to the Lord.

As you and I study the Word and put it into practice, not only will our relationship with God grow and flourish, we will also begin to nurture a closer relationship with our fellow church members and the world.

My challenge to you today is to be a man or a woman who truly knows and loves God's Word. Commit yourself to rightly dividing the Word of truth. Be a Berean rather than a babbler!

chapter 10

The Kind of Person God Uses

2 TIMOTHY 2:20-22

People in the world today are searching high and low for happiness. They read self-help books to try to discover it. They buy tickets to conferences to try to learn the keys to it. They watch Dr. Phil and Oprah every day to try to find it. But, friends, we know the supreme authority for joy and direction in our life is not found in the world; it's found in the Word of God.

Let's turn our attention to what Paul writes in 2 Timothy 2:20–22:

20 Now in a great house there are not only vessels of gold and silver but also of wood and clay, some for honorable use, some for dishonorable. 21 Therefore, if anyone cleanses himself from what is dishonorable, he will be a vessel for honorable use, set apart as holy, useful to the master of the house, ready for every good work.

22 So flee youthful passions and pursue righteousness, faith, love, and peace, along with those who call on the Lord from a pure heart.

Before we go further, we must emphasize the importance of understanding that Paul wrote this letter to those who are already believers. This means that when Paul talks about "a great house," he means the church and he is talking specifically to Christians.

I don't know if your family is like mine, but when I was growing up, spring was the most dreaded time of the year for me. When things started to warm up outside, my parents made us pitch in to help with the spring-cleaning. We started in the house and cleaned everything, and then made our way into the garage and cleaned that too. What we did as a family was to categorize everything into three piles. The first pile was things to keep, the second pile was things to sell, and the third pile was things to throw away.

Examine Your Life for Usefulness

As members of the body of Christ, we need to *examine our lives for usefulness, just as God will one day examine them.* Paul says that within the church, there are vessels to be used for God's purposes. The word *vessel* normally describes an object or utensil. It could be anything that is found in a house. In this specific context, a vessel is a person. Scripture uses this terminology in other places, and Paul uses it in Romans 9:21 to describe the potter and the vessel: "Has the potter no right over the clay, to make out of the same lump a vessel for honorable use and another for dishonorable use?" So we know that *vessel* here refers to a person. Paul also uses this word in 2 Corinthians 4:7 when he writes, "But we have this treasure in jars of clay, to show that the surpassing power belongs to God and not to us."

Within the church body, we find two primary types of vessels. The first type is *honorable vessels* made of gold and silver. Gold vessels are more expensive and more prized than silver, but both are valuable. These vessels are something you put on display, something you want to show other people.

But Paul says that we also find *dishonorable vessels* made of wood and clay. These are inexpensive, ugly, and dirty. Neither type are something that you would be proud to put on display, although wood vessels are more valuable than those made of clay.

Likewise, in the church, there are vessels that are useful to God, and there are vessels that are not so useful to God. Certain vessels grab the attention and serve the Lord openly, and other vessels may be just as useful, but serve the Lord quietly behind the scenes. But unfortunately there are some vessels that are not useful to the Lord at all.

Thankfully, though, God doesn't do exactly what we do when we engage in our spring cleaning. He doesn't just throw us away, even if we're not so useful to Him. Aren't you glad of that? We serve a God who doesn't just discard us, even if we seem to be a not-so-pretty or not-so-useful vessel.

Now, let's explore the context of this letter. The apostle Paul's church had planted Timothy's church. After investing in these men, Paul set up an eldership model for leadership, and invested in the process of discipling Timothy. Then he goes to plan more churches, leaving Timothy with the role of pastor. And as soon as Paul left, division and discord began to occur in the church at Ephesus. The people started grumbling, and, even worse, certain people were sowing false doctrine.

In 1 Timothy, Paul tells Timothy that there were two men in the church that Timothy must get rid of: Alexander and Hymenaeus. He tells Timothy to remove them from the fellowship. And then he mentions two more men in 2 Timothy that need to be removed: Hymenaeus (yes, he was the same man) and Philetus. We're not sure why Hymenaeus was still hanging around, but Paul told Timothy to cleanse his church of these two men. And he goes on to explain to Timothy that in the church, there are vessels of honorable use and dishonorable use.

Cleanse Your Life for Usefulness

Paul teaches that after we examine ourselves for usefulness, we need to *cleanse our lives for usefulness to God.* If we want to be used by God, we have to remove ourselves from those things that could make us dishonorable.

Stay Away from Dishonorable People

The first step in cleansing to cleanse our lives is to *stay away from dishonorable people.* If you want to be used by God, you have to cleanse yourself from people or vessels that are sowing dishonor, discord, and immorality and causing fights and division within the church. Notice that Paul is not talking about people outside of the church; he's talking about people who cause problems *within* the church.

Not only should we refuse to hang around with people who sow discord in the church or teach falsehoods, we also must prevent our minds and hearts from getting caught up in false doctrine. Paul exhorts Timothy to separate himself from false doctrine in the church. He tells him not only to avoid these people, but also to purposefully remove them from the church.

In Proverbs 6:16–19, we read, "There are six things that the LORD hates, seven that are an abomination to him: haughty eyes, a lying tongue, and hands that shed innocent blood, a heart that devises wicked plans, feet that make haste to run to evil, a false witness who breathes out lies, and one who sows discord among brothers."

When people come to me for counseling, whether they are struggling with an addiction to alcohol, drugs, pornography, or any other issue, I always bring them back to the scripture that has become a life verse for me. If you don't know it, it's an excellent one to memorize. First Corinthians 15:33 says in the New International Version: "Bad company corrupts good character." Sinful people will cause good people to sin. As I already mentioned, people who smoke pot cause good people to succumb to temptation and smoke pot. People who go to bars and clubs every Friday and Saturday night eventually will lead good people to go to bars and clubs. People who lie and gossip in the church will cause good people in the church to lie and gossip.

Who are you hanging out with? I'm not just talking about who you spend time with outside of church. Who do you spend time with at church? Are the friends that you associate with vessels of honor and blessing, or are they men and women who sow discord in the body? I don't know about you, but I don't want to hang out with someone who has a corrupt tongue. I don't want to hang out with someone who gossips or engages in godless chatter all the time. I don't want to hang out with someone who has a critical spirit about everyone and everything that crosses their path. I don't want to hang out with someone who has a condemning spirit. I don't want to hang out with someone who is involved in immorality.

Now, this doesn't mean that we should be completely separate from the world and not reach out to people who are involved in these types of lifestyles. Paul says that we need to be *in* the world, but not *of* the world. So it's important for us to remember that while we need to go to the world to save people, we cannot let the world corrupt our value systems and our morals. Paul tells Timothy that if he wants to be used by God, he cannot become entangled with people who cause division. Like Timothy we must keep ourselves pure from the dishonorable vessels."

Here are three characteristics of a person used by God. First of all, he or she will be *sanctified for service*. If you cleanse yourself from dishonorable people and things, you will be a vessel for honorable use. You will be set apart as holy. The process of sanctification does not stop at salvation, it continues on to the end of your life when you reach the final stage of glorification. Justification leads to sanctification; you are set apart as holy your entire life. Then, your earthly life ends with glorification, which means you will get a new body in Christ. What a glorious day that will be! When we abstain from dishonorable people and things, we will be in fellowship with God.

Next, a person used by God will be *equipped for service.* You will be set apart as holy, useful to the master of the house. This word *useful* means "very profitable or very useful." It means readiness: being ready and able to serve the Lord Jesus Christ. Paul says that we should be "equipped for the master of the house." You see, the master of the house has the duty and the right to do whatever he wants with the vessels in the house. God is the Master. He sends you where He wants to send you. You and I are in submission to Him.

Finally, a person used by God will be *prepared for service.* If we are set apart from dishonorable things and dishonorable people, we will be prepared for service. The Greek term means "to be zealous." We should be excited and zealous about serving the Lord Jesus Christ.

Flee Youthful Passions

Paul then tells Timothy that in order to be used by God, he must *flee youthful passions.* This covers much more than just sexual sin. A youthful passion could be chasing worldly success all the time at the cost of your relationships with other people. A youthful passion could be a desire for approval in the workplace or the world. You want to be affirmed by everyone. You're always worried about what everyone else thinks of you. Another youthful passion could be the desire to possess more material wealth. When you get one thing, it's never enough; you always want more, bigger, and better. Another youthful passion would be the desire for recognition. You want to be the most handsome, the prettiest, the smartest, the fastest, the richest, or the most successful. You want people to approve of you. Another youthful passion is the desire to have everything you want *now.* It's a lack of patience, an inability to wait upon the Lord.

As believers, we need to stand firm against the enemy, but when it comes to sin, we need to run headlong in the other direction. You don't need to meddle in or mingle with sin. Run away from it; don't look to see how it's going to pan out.

Holiness is a requirement for our usefulness to God. Did you know that? If you want to be used by God, you have to be a holy vessel. Paul wanted to drive this point home so much so that he bookends or sandwiches this concept of vessels between two commands to stay holy. Look at 2 Timothy 2:19: "But God's firm foundation stands bearing this seal: 'The Lord knows those who are his.' Let everyone who names the name of the Lord depart from iniquity." He bookends this concept with *seek holiness*, and then look at verse 22: "So flee youthful passions and pursue righteousness, faith, love, and peace." Paul is saying, "If you want to be a vessel for honorable use, you've got to be holy."

Friends, are you seeking after holiness in your life? Are you fleeing youthful passions? Are you getting caught up in the desires of the world?

Pursue the Lord

Paul reminds Timothy that if he wants to be used by God, then he will have to run away from these things. Thankfully, we can't run away from something without running to something. And that brings me to Paul's third point: *pursue the Lord*. Paul instructs Timothy to run away from sin as fast and as far as he can, and to run toward the Lord. Like Timothy, we can do this by focusing on four biblical virtues.

The first virtue is righteousness. or right standing, conduct, and ethical behavior with God. Psalm 119:9 shows us how we can pursue righteousness, "How can a man keep his way pure? By guarding it according to your word." You see, when we know the Word of God and love the Word of God and live the Word of God, we begin to pursue righteousness. I heard another pastor say, "When you work the Word, the Word works in your life." That's the idea Paul is trying to convey. When we get into the Word until the Word gets into us, we begin to pursue right standing and living before the Lord.

Let me ask you this: do you pursue faith? In this context, *faith* is better rendered as *faithfulness*. It's the same word that is used in Galatians

5:22 when Paul writes about the fruit of the Spirit: "For the fruit of the Spirit is love, joy, peace, patience, kindness, goodness, faithfulness, gentleness, self-control." A hermeneutical principle I learned from Dr. Dwight Pryor is that if you want to know the meaning of a word in any part of the Bible, go back to the first time that word is used in scripture. Jewish people will say that the first time God gives a word to the Jews, it has an overarching theme for the rest of the Bible. Guess where the word *faithfulness* is first used in the Bible? Exodus chapter 17. The word *faithfulness* in Exodus 17 is the word *emunah*. *Emunah* means "steady."

In biblical language, faith is a verb, not a noun. As believers in Jesus Christ, we must pursue faithfulness to the Lord. We need to be faithful to God in every aspect of our lives. Not only that, but we must also pursue love. . That word *love* is an interesting word. Paul chooses an opportune moment to tell Timothy, "Yes, I know the church is difficult. Yes, I know that you have sinners in the church. Yes, I know that people are causing division. But Timothy, you need to love those who don't love you. You need to do as God did. Jesus said, 'You love me because I first loved you.'"

Agape love is love that is selfless. Agape love is not tied to emotions. Agape love is not transactional; it doesn't mean that I return your love because of something you did for me. It's unconditional love, loving someone even though they don't love you. It's loving someone who is unlovable. Is there someone in your life that you need to show unconditional love to?

Finally, we need to *pursue peace*. Peace is where we get the word for serenity. It's the opposite of war and combat and fighting and strife. It's the word *shalom,* from which we get our terms "wholeness" or "completeness." It means inner peace and a harmonious relationship between God and man. Honorable vessels pursue peace.

Are you pursuing righteousness in your life, or are you living like a dishonorable vessel that is not being used by God? Do you want to be useful to the Master of the great house, ready for every good work? If so, then this is what you must take a look at the landscape of your life and decide if you are hanging out with people who are dishonorable. Ask yourself if you are getting caught up in dishonorable things. If you are, then you need to stop. Let's be about the business of pursuing righteousness, faith, love, and peace.

Reject Controversies

Fourth, in order to cleanse yourself and be a vessel God can use, you must *reject controversies*. Paul writes, "Have nothing to do with foolish, ignorant controversies; you know that they breed quarrels." He mentions this a number of times in various letters. He wrote in 1 Timothy 4:7, "Timothy, have nothing to do with irreverent, silly myths. Rather train yourself for godliness." He also wrote in Titus 3:10–11: "As for a person who stirs up division, after warning him once and then twice, have nothing more to do with him, knowing that such a person is warped and sinful; he is self condemned."

We are being commanded here to avoid foolish things. The Greek word translated *foolish* is the word *moras*, meaning "dull, stupid, or silly." It's the root from which we get the English word *moron*. Paul is saying, "Don't get involved in undisciplined, uneducated, unbiblical arguments. Stay away from moronic talk."

Too many people in our churches today get involved in foolish, ignorant controversies. I'm sure you know people who have been involved in foolish talk that was not profitable for those involved or for the church as a whole. Most of the time, this type of talk is based on people or things we don't like. We don't like the way they look, sound, or act, or we don't like the way something was done. It's normally a matter of personal preference.

As a pastor, I love my church, and I love it for a number of reasons. But one of the main reasons is that it is made up of believers who say, "We're going to put aside our personal preferences in order to serve God. We're going to have an attitude of valuing 'we over me.' We realize that some things may be said and done that we may not agree with, but for the sake of the church, and for the sake of the glory of God and our desire to reach the nations, we are going to put aside our preferences to maintain unity in the body."

Sadly, in many churches, people fight over things that are temporal, which results in division. They do this at the expense of the lost people in the community. While they focus on petty things, people all around them are dying and going to hell for eternity.

Friends, it's time for the church of the Lord Jesus Christ to wake up and realize we need to put our personal preferences aside in order to avoid engaging in foolish, ignorant arguments. We live in a world where millions of people are dying of poverty and sickness and depression and emptiness and neglect and addiction and hunger and sin, and we have no time to waste. In fact, we have no time to argue unless it is a biblical argument.

Paul wants to be sure that Timothy is aware that people in the church will cause confrontation It may seems as if he is belaboring the point, as if Timothy is not getting it. Paul says in 1 Timothy 4, "Have nothing to do with foolish, silly myths." Then he says it again in 2 Timothy: "Have nothing to do with foolish, irreverent controversies; you know that they breed quarrels." Why does he keep telling Timothy this? Because Timothy will continue to run into these controversies, and Paul wants to remind him to remove the "dishonorable vessels" and then let God handle the problem.

Most important, Paul wants Timothy to continue to focus on the main thing—to unashamedly preach the gospel of the Lord Jesus Christ. We can make sure that we are honorable vessels by doing the same: rightly dividing the Word of truth and seeking holiness.

chapter 11

Sharing the Message
of New Life in Christ

2 TIMOTHY 2:23-26

As we strive to become honorable vessels that God can use, we need to focus on two actions: evangelizing effectively and relying on God for the results. Let's explore 2 Timothy 2:23–26 to find out how to do this.

> 23 Have nothing to do with foolish, ignorant controversies; you know that they breed quarrels. 24 And the Lord's servant must not be quarrelsome but kind to everyone, able to teach, patiently enduring evil, 25 correcting his opponents with gentleness. God may perhaps grant them repentance leading to a knowledge of the truth, 26 and they may come to their senses and escape from the snare of the devil, after being captured by him to do his will.

Evangelize Effectively

First, you and I must be committed to *evangelizing effectively*. We see this in verse 25, where the focus is placed on God granting sinners repentance. We've already discussed how you preach the gospel every day without ever saying a word. People are watching you to see if your words and actions are Christlike or not.

It's interesting that Paul doesn't directly challenge Timothy to do the things listed in verses 24 through 26; he simply describes what the Lord's servant should say and do. He says, "This is what a wise servant of the Lord looks like." His point is that the way Timothy lives will either lead people toward Christ or away from Christ. When people look at your life, knowing that you are a follower of the Lord, they should be able to clearly see Christ-like characteristics in your life.

You may be wondering how you can know whether or not you possess these characteristics. Here's a great way to find out. Ask your wife. Ask your husband. Ask your parents. Ask your friends or other church members. Paul directs us to four main characteristics that will be present in the life of the person who is living like Christ.

Be Kind to Others

Paul begins by again stressing his instruction to Timothy that those in the church avoid quarreling. Then he stresses that the Lord's servant should *be kind to others*. "And the Lord's servant must not be quarrelsome but kind to everyone." The word *kind* is not a verb; it's an adjective describing a person. A person who is kind is also gracious and mild. In his first letter to the church at Thessalonica, in chapter 2, verse 7, Paul tells them, "but we were gentle among you like a nursing mother taking care of her own children" (NIV). Is it safe to say a nursing mother is gentle to her beloved children and to other people? You and I need to be just as gentle. Paul tells the church at Corinth in 2 Corinthians 10:1:

"I, Paul, myself, entreat you by the meekness and gentleness of Christ." A kind person is the opposite of quarrelsome.

Be Skilled in Teaching

In addition to being kind, you need to be *skilled in teaching*. This means you must be able to effectively communicate the Word of God. I know that Paul is talking to Timothy, and you may be saying, "But I'm not a teacher by vocation. I'm not gifted in that way." While it's true that teaching may not come naturally to everyone, we can all work at improving our capabilities in this area. Remember you are constantly teaching yourself every day.

Recently, in an expository teaching class at my church, I asked the students, "What do you want to get out of this class?"

One of the men in the class said, "I want to learn how to teach myself the Bible." What a great goal! We can all grow and improve in our ability to teach so that we can have a more powerful spiritual influence on our families and our friends.

Paul is not saying, "Timothy, you must learn vast amounts of information and be able to speak on all kinds of different topics." He's not saying, "Fill your mind with knowledge simply for the sake of having that knowledge." Rather, he's saying that a believer in Timothy's position must be a man of God who knows how to handle the scriptures properly, rightly dividing the Word of truth in order to teach God's people how to live.

Be Patient When Wronged

Third, Paul says, you must *be patient when wronged*. Up to this point, I'm sure you've been agreeing with me. Yes, I know we need to be kind to others. Yes, I know we need to be skilled in teaching. But this command is a bit harder for us to swallow, right? We have a hard time being patient with people who do us wrong, especially when it is something that happens repeatedly. When other people hurt us, we may feel like saying, "Hey, I believe in the Old Testament, brother: an eye for an eye and a tooth for a tooth."

But Paul tells Timothy, "Listen, there will be times when people in the church will rise up against you and speak out against you and try to hurt you, and you need to be patient with them." This word *patient* means "to be tolerant" or "to bear evil" for the sake and the purpose of the gospel.

The apostle Peter gives us an insight on this concept in 1 Peter 2:21–22. Peter uses an illustration from the life of Christ: "For to this you have been called, because Christ also suffered for you, leaving you an example so that you might follow in his steps. He committed no sin, neither was deceit found in his mouth."

Of all the words that Paul could have used for *patience* in the New Testament, he chooses a word that appears only once in the entire Bible. This particular Greek word is found only in this passage. Paul didn't use the word for perseverance, he didn't use the word for longsuffering, and he didn't use the word for forbearing. This special word for patience means, "to be patient with someone you love." Pretty surprising, considering that the context is describing divisive people in the church who are rising up and trying to attack the servant of the Lord.

It's easy to be patient with people in the world, because they're lost. But how easy is it to be patient with a spouse who constantly degrades you when you go to church? How easy is it to be patient with a person whom you love who has fallen into false teaching or false doctrine? Paul is warning Timothy that these things will happen and that the servant of God must continue to be patient.

Paul also teaches that we need to be patient with a purpose. If every time you go to church your spouse puts you down for following Christ, you just be patient. Young people, when you're at school and people make fun of you for following Jesus, you just be patient with them. If you have coworkers at the office who constantly criticize you and persecute you for your beliefs, be patient with them with a purpose. When we are patient with a purpose, our gentleness disciplines those who are sinning.

Peter writes about Jesus in 1 Peter 2:23, "When he was reviled, he did not revile in return; when he suffered, he did not threaten, but continued entrusting himself to him who judges justly."

Discipline with Gentleness

Jesus may not have gone looking for a fight, but he did correct people when they were wrong. Yet He did so with a spirit of love and gentleness.

Paul also tells Timothy that he needed to discipline or correct with gentleness. We need to gently guide those who are childlike in their faith, or who are mature and still need to grow. This is the same word used to describe the process of instructing a child. Paul exhorts Timothy to deal gently with Christians who are childlike in their maturity.

Just because you may be an older person in the church doesn't mean that you are necessarily spiritually mature. Age does not equal maturity. Whether we are young, old, or in between, we need to be on both the giving and the receiving ends of discipline. When you confront someone for being theologically or biblically wrong, you are showing them God's love. Paul says you need to do this with gentleness. We also need to accept correction with a spirit of gentleness when others hold us accountable.

Paul needed to remind Timothy to be gentle with his discipline because so many of those in his church were spiritual babies. Hebrews 5:11 says,

> About this we have much to say, and it is hard to explain, since you have become dull of hearing. For though by this time you ought to be teachers, you need someone to teach you again the basic principles of the oracles of God. You need milk, not solid food, for everyone who lives on milk is unskilled in the word of righteousness, since he is a child. But solid food is for the mature, for

those who have their powers of discernment trained by constant practice to distinguish good from evil.

Paul and Timothy knew that they needed to confront false teaching in the church with gentleness and meekness. Now, don't miss this. *Meekness* does not mean *weakness*. Here is the perfect example: Jesus was meek, but He was certainly not weak. Twice, Jesus cleansed the temple of corruption. He blasted the hypocrites. He condemned the false leaders of Israel. He fearlessly uttered God's divine judgment upon certain people. And the Bible says he was meek and gentle, using His power only for the defense of God's plan and kingdom purposes.

The Greek philosopher Aristotle said, "This word for meekness is in the middle of two extremes. On the one hand you have getting angry without reason; and on the other hand you have not getting angry at all."[18] Meekness or gentleness is right in the middle. A meek person will get angry at the right time, in the right measure, for the right reason. A meek person will say, "I'll never defend myself, but I will die defending God." That's spiritual meekness.

Former U.S. president Teddy Roosevelt said it this way: "Walk softly and carry a big stick." Be meek and gentle, but be prepared to give help or support to the things you really believe in.

You don't want to go out and cause trouble for people. You don't want to confront people unnecessarily. But if someone is blaspheming the name of God, putting down Christ, or teaching falsehoods in the church, you have the right and the duty as a believer to confront that person in love. "Hey, brother, listen, I love you, but you're wrong to say or do that. Don't take my word for it; let me show you what the Bible says."

This is why Paul says over and over that false teaching within the body of Christ will spread like gangrene. If we don't step in and stand up for God's truth when the circumstances call for it, false teaching and division could ruin the church.

Rely on God for the Results

Finally, Paul says, *rely on God for the results of your evangelism.* There are two parts to this: repentance and obedience.

God Grants Repentance

First of all, we must recognize that *God is the one who grants repentance.* It's the Lord who enables a lost person to see the error of his ways and come to his senses. That's the only way a nonbeliever can escape the snare of the devil.

This repentance happens by God's sovereignty, according to His grace. Paul was a man who believed in the sovereignty of God. He knew that no matter what happened, God was still in control. He proclaimed this truth all through the book of 2 Timothy.

There is more to repentance than just giving up a behavior or attitude. Repentance is realizing that you're traveling too fast down a dead-end street, headed for destruction, caught up in your sin and yourself. But when God gets a hold of you, you suddenly realize that you have to turn around. You must do a 180-degree turn and completely, radically change your mind about sin. Instead of rationalizing it, instead of trying to cover it up, instead of making excuses for it, you agree with God about your sin. You learn to see it the way He does.

You don't say, "Oh, I'm not really that bad. Compared to so-and-so, I'm actually pretty good." If you want to compare yourself to somebody, compare yourself to Christ. When you look into the face of Christ and realize His perfect standard and the suffering He experienced due to your sin, you will understand why we all need to repent. There's not a person in this world who does not need to repent, including me as a pastor. All of us have times in our life when we need to not only turn around but also completely change the way we view sin. We have to learn to see it from the vantage point of God's standard—perfection. And we can't measure up.

We are sinful human beings. How can a sinful human being really change his or her mind about sin? Tyring to repent on your own is like taking a bath in mud. No matter how much effort you put into it, it really doesn't do anything to get you clean, The same thing goes for repentance. That's why Paul says *God is the one who grants repentance.*

Believers Must Obey God's Word

God grants repentance, but it's our responsibility as believers to *obey His Word*. When God grants repentance, that leads us to knowledge of the truth. The knowledge of the truth is not mere intellectual assent; it's not learning all the doctrines of the faith so you can check off a few boxes; it's not filling your mind with information or factual knowledge. True knowledge is knowing Christ.

Jesus says in John 8, "You will know the truth, and the truth will set you free." He also writes, "In the beginning was the Word, and the Word was with God, and the Word was God. And the Word became flesh and dwelt among us" (John 1:1, 14). Jesus is the Word that he speaks of, the embodiment of the truth. When we study the Word and we repent of our sin, God grants repentance. Repentance brings us to our senses, allowing us to escape the snare of the devil after he has tried to capture us to do his will.

In Greek, the term that is translated "comes to their senses" is an amazing word. It actually describes the process of an alcoholic sobering up, the way a person who has been possessed or controlled by something else (not in his or her right mind, acting contrary to his or her own will) sobers up and is suddenly in his or her right mind again.

When we are able to do this, Paul says, we will escape the snare of the devil. Did you know that people in churches all over the world have been captured and hijacked by the devil? A person who is belligerent, a person who is argumentative, a person who is quarrelsome as a believer may have been misled or captured by the devil. Paul tells us that we must correct this person with gentleness. If he still doesn't turn from his ways, we should avoid him.

You may think that Paul is being harsh, but the truth is that there are people in the church whose minds and hearts seem to have been captured by the devil. There are dishonorable people. There are divisive people. There are immoral people. These people must be treated with gentleness.

I believe this passage drove Timothy to his knees. God is the judge, and He is the only one who grants repentance. God cleanses and uses the vessel. God orchestrates salvation. He is the author, initiator, finisher, and perfecter of our faith. We must beg God to move in our lives and in the lives of others in our church.

On my own, I can't cause you to repent. I can preach on repentance, I can challenge you to repent, but if God doesn't grant you repentance, you will never repent. That's why we all need to be about the business of praying to God. Paul wrote in Philippians 1:6, "I am sure of this, that he who began a good work in you will bring it to completion at the day of Christ Jesus." God is the only one with the power to begin and complete a good work in us.

Aren't you glad that God doesn't leave us in our sin?

It's easy to feel like we couldn't possibly be the person in the church who has been captured by the devil, but the truth is that no one is immune to his deception. Usually the person who has been deceived is the last one to know. Thankfully, God gives us a way out. First Corinthians 10:13 says, "God is faithful. He will not let you be tempted beyond your ability, but with the temptation he will also provide the way of escape." Aren't you glad of that? First John 1:9 says, "If we confess our sins, he is faithful and just to forgive us our sins and to cleanse us from all unrighteousness."

I want to challenge you today: if you have been misled or captured by the devil, if you're in the snare of the enemy, would you please ask God for repentance? Would you confess your sin to God and say, "God, forgive me"? All of us need to do this. We're all sinners. We're all a work in progress. You and I have a choice every day—are we going to serve the Lord, or are we going to serve ourselves? We must remember that the same vessel can be used for honor or dishonor.

The great painter Leonardo da Vinci realized as he was preparing to paint the Christ figure in his painting *The Last Supper* that he needed a portrait model who exemplified the qualities of Christ. He wanted someone who looked almost like an angel. So he went to a church in Rome where he found an angelic-looking young choirboy named Pietro Bandinelli. He asked this young boy to come and sit in his studio while he painted his face as the face of Jesus. Afterward, da Vinci said, "Pietro, thank you for your help." And the boy left.

Leonardo da Vinci put that painting on the back burner for many years. He completed some other works. Later in his life, he decided that he really wanted to finish *The Last Supper* painting. He realized that he had painted every person in the scene except Judas Iscariot.

Leonardo realized that in order to paint Judas, he had to find someone whose face was hardened, someone who had the look of evil, someone who had been beaten down by life with a face that was somehow disfigured or corrupted. So he went out and started walking the streets of Rome. He found a homeless man, a man who clearly had lived a difficult, painful life. He asked this homeless man to come into his studio so that he could paint his face. And he did. Even as Leonardo was painting this man's face, it was hard to look at him. This man had weathered many storms in life.

After Leonardo had finished painting the man's face, he thanked him and told him he was free to go. But he said, "Before you leave, what is your name, so I know who you are?"

The homeless man said, "My name is Pietro Bandinelli. You painted me when I was a child. I'm the face of Christ in the same painting."[19]

I want to ask you today, what road are you going down? The same vessel that was once used for honor can later be used for dishonor. The same face that once reflected Christ can lose its joy and its light. Do you want to please God? Do you want to be used by God? If you do, you need to examine your life. You need to cleanse your life for usefulness. You need to evangelize effectively by sharing the gospel through your words and your actions, then let God reap the results.

Everywhere you go, people should notice that there's something different about you—that your life reflects the qualities and characteristics of Christ.

chapter 12

Increasing Discernment in an Undiscerning World

2 TIMOTHY 3:1-9

In this chapter, I'd like to address a topic that is very important to the church as a whole. I want to explore some of the ways that we can increase our discernment in an undiscerning world. This will help us avoid the three deadly dangers that threaten to hinder our discipleship mission.

In 1988, the evangelical philosopher and theologian Carl Henry wrote a book about the future of our country called *The Twilight of a Great Civilization*. He says that America is progressively losing its Judeo-Christian heritage. As we lose touch with our spiritual heritage and values, our nation continues to become more pagan. He says, "Given the present historical dynamisms, my view is that in another half generation—before the turn of the century—humanism will have lost its humanism and the regenerate Church will survive in the social context of naked naturalism and raw paganism."[20] He compares the challenges of the twenty-first-century believers with struggles the first-century Christians faced against Rome and the world.

It's safe to say, friends, we are seeing the reality of what Carl Henry wrote about more than twenty years ago. Don't you believe that we're living in the last days? But, since Paul prophesied two thousand years ago what would happen, we should not be alarmed.

From time to time, people ask me, "Are you alarmed at what's happening today?"

I say, "No, I'm not alarmed. I expect it, because Paul talked about it."

That's what I want to share with you today. In 2 Timothy 3:1–9, Paul warns Timothy about the difficult days ahead. He was writing two thousand years ago not about something in our future, but about spiritual conditions that are a present reality in our society today. In 2 Timothy 3 Paul writes:

> 1 But understand this, that in the last days there will come times of difficulty. 2 For people will be lovers of self, lovers of money, proud, arrogant, abusive, disobedient to their parents, ungrateful, unholy, 3 heartless, unappeasable, slanderous, without self-control, brutal, not loving good, 4 treacherous, reckless, swollen with conceit, lovers of pleasure rather than lovers of God, 5 having the appearance of godliness, but denying its power. Avoid such people. 6 For among them are those who creep into households and capture weak women, burdened with sins and led astray by various passions, 7 always learning and never able to arrive at a knowledge of the truth. 8 Just as Jannes and Jambres opposed Moses, so these men also oppose the truth, men corrupted in mind and disqualified regarding the faith. 9 But they will not get very far, for their folly will be plain to all, as was that of those two men.

Paul tells us that the last days will be a time of great difficulty. The Greek word *difficulty* is the word for "stress" or "agony." When Paul tells Timothy "understand this," the word "understand" means "to perceive" or "to be continually about the business of looking and observing and waiting and watching so you don't get caught off guard." Let's explore some of the reasons Paul would stress the importance of understanding the last days according to this definition.

Counterfeit Christians

Three dangers lurk in our churches that have the ability to sidetrack us from our mission. The first one is this: *counterfeit Christians*. Paul tells us that there are people in the church who look like Christians, but are not. I've seen this in the church myself, and, most likely, you have too.

What are the reasons for the difficult times in the last days? Well, Paul describes tells us in verse 2: "*For people will be lovers of self*" (emphasis added). The reason for this corruption is the counterfeit Christians within the church. Good and bad, sheep and goats. Paul says, "You need to be wary of these people."

John Stott says, "It is important to grasp that it is men who are responsible for the menacing seasons which the church has to bear, fallen men, evil men, men whose nature is perverted, whose behavior is self-centered and godless, whose mind is hostile to God and His law, and who spread evil, heresy, and dead religion in the church."[21]

A Moral Condition

These counterfeit Christians possess two characteristics that should help you identify them. First, they possess *a moral condition*. Look at the first characteristic. *For men will be lovers of self.* This one phrase is the overarching theme, my friends, for the next eighteen or nineteen qualities that follow.

Lovers of silver. That's exactly what its saying. Lovers of self. Lovers of silver. Or, lovers of money. Did you know that the Pharisees were actually lovers of money? Jesus says it in Luke chapter 16, verse 14: "The

Pharisees and Scribes loved money." Now listen, money is not bad, but the love of money is evil. That's what Paul tells Timothy.

Proud. This word *proud* is the word for boasting in oneself. Boasting in itself is not necessarily wrong. Paul says in 1 Corinthians 1:31, "let he who boasts, boast the Lord." Here in 2 Timothy it is the idea of being arrogant, of being abusive to one another or other people. Again, this pride in one's own accomplishments relates back to the love of self described at the beginning of the passage.

The next five characteristics in the text—disobedient to parents, ungrateful, unholy, unappeasable, and heartless—have the word with the letter "a" in front of it in the Greek. When the letter "a" appears in front of a word, it implies a negation. Atheism means no God. Agnosticism— "a" in front of "gnostic"—means no knowledge. It would be similar to you and I putting the prefix "dis" in front of a word. Dissatisfied means you are not satisfied. It's the opposite of what you should seek. So the person should be holy, the person should be grateful, the person should be obedient, but they're not.

A good example of someone in the Bible who was disobedient to his parents is seen in the story of the prodigal son, found in Luke 15. He went to his father and spiritually slapped him in the face, saying, "I want my money now." He could have bankrupted the family, but he demanded what he wanted anyway. He took his money, and, according to the New American Standard Bible, he blew that money on "loose living." Once he experienced a life of destitution, he came back to his father, having realized that he was ungrateful, that he was unholy, that he was disobedient, and that his sin was unappeasable, and he asked his father and God to forgive him. What a great story to help us classify and categorize these immoral character traits.

Look at the next traits. Slanderous. This is another word for being devilish. It means without self-control, brutal, not loving good. The King James Bible translates this as "incontinent, fierce, despisers of those that are good."

The next characteristic listed is "treacherous." The person who is treacherous is a traitor. It's the same word used in Luke chapter 6 when Luke says Judas Iscariot was a traitor. The final characteristic listed is swollen with conceite. Like the other conditions, this is a moral deficit that involves pride and, once again, a love for self.

A Religious Condition

Not only do counterfeit Christians possess a moral condition, they also possess *a religious condition*. This is a more subtle way to identify them. Paul describes these people as "lovers of pleasure rather than lovers of God, having the appearance of godliness, but denying its power." That Greek term *lovers of pleasure* is where we get the English word *hedonism*. It's the idea of a person bent on seeking pleasure and excitement in the world. It's not necessarily wrong to seek pleasure; we want to have pleasure in God. In Psalm 37:4, the psalmist writes, "Delight yourself in the LORD, and he will give you the desires of your heart." But the person Paul refers to is focused only on serving self. Paul is simply saying that we should not elevate the pursuit of pleasure over the pursuit of God.

God's order is plainly declared in His moral law. We're called to love Him first with all our heart, all our mind, all our soul, and all our strength; love our neighbors second; and love ourselves last. God, neighbor, self. Whenever our view of self is too highly elevated, everything around us is affected. If you're on the throne of your life today and God is not, there's a problem. Ask yourself, "Do I love Jesus and think about Him first, or do I love myself and put myself first?"

Godly humility is not thinking less of oneself; it's thinking of Christ first. Is God on the throne of your life, or are you on the throne? Because if you are sitting there on the throne, as pretty as you please, you may have a religious and moral condition like the counterfeit Christians. These counterfeit Christians looked like believers, but they were secretly serving themselves rather than God.

Corrupt Relationships

The second danger in the church is this: *corrupt relationships.* Paul tells us that these people will have the appearance of godliness, but they will deny its power." It can be hard to identify this kind of person in the church. They may do and say all the right things.

Paul tells Titus in Titus 1:16 that some people in the church will profess to know God and claim to follow Him, but will deny his by their deeds. He goes on to tell us that are detestable and disobedient and worthless for any good deed." These religious leaders may pretend to serve the Lord. They may masquerade as Christians, but secretly they are serving self, and they are corrupting the church.

In today's words, Jesus might say it this way: "It's not the outward appearance that matters; it's the subtle sin of the heart that reveals the true spiritual nature of a person" (see 1 Samuel 16:7). You can act like a Christian on the outside, and, inwardly, you can be of the devil.

Paul gives an indication that these dangerous people will be tough to spot in the church. They will look godly, but inwardly they will deny His power. In the New Testament Judas was able to fool even the disciples.

Let me show you two instances where Judas practiced this deception. John 12:3 describes a scene in which Jesus and the disciples are all reclining at the table: "Mary therefore took a pound of expensive ointment made from pure nard, and anointed the feet of Jesus and wiped his feet with her hair." I preached a sermon on this about how Mary has her own worship service with the Lord. She brought forth a bottle of ointment of great value, broke the bottle, bowed down on her knees, and blessed the Lord Jesus Christ by anointing Him for burial and wiping His feet with her hair. She loved Jesus so much that she was willing to humble herself and have a worship service in front of all these apostles.

Many scholars believe that this vessel of precious ointment could have cost the equivalent of $30,000 today. Yes, you read that right! That's a lot of money. Mary broke open this vessel, and the beautiful fragrance filled the room. Everybody enjoyed the moment but one person. Look at Judas's response in verses 4 and 5: "But Judas Iscariot, one of his disciples (he who was about to betray him), said, 'Why was this ointment not sold for three hundred denarii and given to the poor?'"

If you and I had been there, we might have said, "Wow, Judas, you're right! You really have a heart for missions. You are so spiritual! Thanks for looking out for the less fortunate, brother." But Judas was not intent on taking the gospel to the nationsor focused on worshiping Christ. Judas seemed to be envious of all the attention Jesus was getting. He wanted to turn the focus onto himself and be praised for being so "thoughtful." He wanted to be worshiped. Do you see the subtle hints of this in the text?

That brings me back to a crucial point: there are people in our churches today who are disguising themselves as godly. These individuals attend church services. They might teach Sunday school or work in the nursery. They might even be deacons or elders in the church. They might be high-profile people in the community who say they follow the Lord Jesus. They might even pray and read their Bibles. They might give to the church; yet, their hearts are not in the right place. They are lost.

Keep in mind that I'm not talking about individual believers who have a momentary lapse of sin. That's not what I'm saying. None of us is perfect. I'm talking about people who seem to do all of the right things but their hearts actually do not belong to the Lord. They are corrupt. They are bent habitually on sin, and they are not born again. It is these people that Paul warns us about.

Here's the opposite extreme: looking at someone who doesn't appear godly on the outside and criticizing that person. I hear this all the time: "Pastor, can you believe what such-and-such wore to church on Sunday? What about that guy with all those tattoos? Did you see that teenager with the pink hair sitting in the back row? I can't believe she would even darken the door of our church!" The people saying such things are critical in their hearts and judgmental in their spirits. They think that a person's outward appearance reflects his or her inner heart condition.

Did you ever think about the fact that Jesus hung out with people who were outwardly sinful at the expense of hanging out with those who were outwardly religious? Jesus spent most of his time with the tax collectors, the prostitutes, the drug addicts, the adulterers, the murderers, and the sinners. He did not hang out with the religious leaders who appeared to have it all together on the outside but, inwardly, did not have hearts that loved God. Jesus did not hang out with the Pharisees or Sadducees, who quoted scripture, wore fancy clothes, and walked around looking pious.

Why did Jesus prefer to spend His time with those who recognized their sin? Because He was not looking at appearance; He was looking at the heart. He realized that even though the down and out people of His society did not look religious, they had a desire for Him. They wanted to know the truth. They wanted to be saved from their sin.

Friends, we've got to be careful about judging people. Appearances are deceptive. Jesus knew that, and Paul knew it too. That's why Paul says, "Avoid such people." That Greek term *avoid* is the word for literally "taking yourself by the collar and dragging yourself out of a situation." When you're tempted to sin, take yourself by the collar and drag yourself away. Remove yourself from these people.

Now, I'm not talking about church discipline here. Church discipline is only exercised against believers; these men were unbelievers in the church. Corrupting relationships will lead a church away from its mission.

Crooked Leaders and Teachers

The third danger in the church is caused by *crooked leaders and teachers*. Paul describes these people as "those who creep into households and capture weak women, burdened with sins and led astray by various passions."

How They Approach

Let me show you four things about these crooked leaders and teachers. First, I want to show you *how they approach* in a secretive manner. That word *capture* is a military term; it means to sneak up on someone and take him or her as a prisoner of war. If you've ever been in the military, you know the process of taking a prisoner of war. This Greek term has the connotation of "being captured secretly or covertly, not openly." That's exactly the agenda of these false teachers. They don't capture people openly; they do it secretly and seductively.

Bishop Ellicott says it this way: "This method is as old as the fall of man. For the serpent first deceived Eve, it was employed by the Gnostics in John's time and beyond, and it has been a regular ploy of religious commercial travelers right up to and including the Jehovah's Witnesses of our day."[22]

Who They Assault

Second, whom do these people assault? The passage says that they seek "weak women." Now, Paul mentions only women, but I believe that this applies to weak men as well. Crooked leaders seek people who are weak in their faith. These people have two problems. The first problem is that they are *morally weak*. The text says they are "burdened with sins and led astray by various passions." Another translation says "They are loaded down with sins and led away by various lusts" (NKJV).

In contrast, Paul told Timothy in 2 Timothy 2:22 to "flee youthful passions and pursue righteousness, faith, love, and peace, along with those who call on the Lord from a pure heart." He warns Timothy and his readers of the dangers of being led astray by youthful passions. And the word "passions" doesn't just mean sexual passions; it can mean any passion or lust that you have for something other than God.

R. Kent Hughes writes, "The women's conscience was burdened and thus, they gave ready ears to imposters who promised to ease their guilt. Their unconfessed sin stood between them and God and made their reasoning faulty; their sins like an especially violent flu left them vulnerable to the worse of diseases."[23]

We mentioned that these people were morally weak. In addition, they were *mentally weak*. Sin plagued their minds. We have to remember that the devil is subtle. He will come in secretly and blind the eyes of unbelievers so they can't see their sin and can't recognize the truth. These people were going from false teaching to false teaching, following false teacher after false teacher. They were constantly seeking but never able to arrive at knowledge of the truth.

In 2009, there was a public hearing about a group of Mormons in Utah. They all gathered together at the town hall because they wanted to legalize polygamy. News reporters performed interviews with several members of the crowd, and they found out that one of the Mormon men had twelve wives. Can you imagine that? Twelve wives.

A girl named Christine was one of the women interviewed. She said, "My relationship with my husband is only going to be great if his relationship with his other wives is great." She goes on to say: "I have such a wonderful husband. I am so privileged. He is such a blessing that I am willing to share him with other women." My question is this: how does a person get to the point where she is so deceived that she thinks that it's actually okay to share her husband with eleven other women? You can only get to that point by being subtly led astray from false teaching and being burdened with sin. That's the mindset Paul is referring to in this passage.

Why They Attack

We must also notice why these crooked teachers attack. Paul gives the example of Jannes and Jambres. If you're not sure who these men are, you're not alone. In fact, nowhere else in the Bible do we find the names of these two men.

According to Jewish tradition, Jannes and Jambres are the magicians mentioned in Exodus chapter 7. Do you remember the story of Moses and Aaron approaching Pharaoh? In today's words, God says to Moses, "Tell Aaron to take his staff and throw it on the ground." He did, and it became a snake. But the magicians in the courtyard that day did the same thing. They mirrored God. They took a staff, threw it down on the ground, and it turned into a snake too. Every time Aaron and Moses did something, these magicians, who many believe were named Jannes and Jambres, imitated and mimicked the things of God.

Paul's point is that we, like Timothy, will encounter people in the church—men and women—who will actually mimic the things of God, but they are of the devil. He says, "Just as Jannes and Jambres opposed Moses, so these men also oppose the truth."

Why do they oppose the truth? Because they had been blinded by the devil. These men were fake believers. They acted as if they were of God, but they were not of God.

In Romans 1:18–21, Paul writes,

> For the wrath of God is revealed from heaven against all ungodliness and unrighteousness of men, who by their unrighteousness suppress the truth. For what can be known about God is plain to them, because God has shown it to them. For his invisible attributes, namely, his eternal power and divine nature, have been clearly perceived, ever since the creation of the world, in the things that have been made. So they are without excuse. For although they knew God, they did not honor him as God or give thanks to him, but they became futile in their thinking, and their foolish hearts were darkened.

These men don't know God because they have suppressed the truth with their wickedness. They are depraved in their minds.

In 2 Corinthians 11:13, Paul describes such people as "false apostles, deceitful workmen, disguising themselves as apostles of Christ." In this case, the false teachers didn't just describe themselves as followers of

UNASHAMED

Christ; they went around claiming to be apostles, but they were actually of the devil. "And no wonder," verse 14 continues "for even Satan disguises himself as an angel of light."

How They Will Be Apprehended

Paul's closes this passage by telling us *how they will be apprehended*. Paul tells Timothy, "These crooked teachers will not get very far, for their folly will be plain to all."

In the end, these men will be exposed. You and I both know examples of pastors and preachers who had ministries around the world but were involved in sin, and, eventually, their sin was exposed. I'm not going to name them because you know who they are.

Here's the point: you and I, as members of the church of the Lord Jesus Christ, need to understand the signs of the times. We need to understand the day and age in which we live so that we can identify counterfeit Christians, identify the corrupting relationships in the church and outside the church, and identify the crooked leaders in order to preserve our church and protect ourselves. That's why Paul says in 2 Corinthians 13:5, as he closes that letter, "Examine yourselves." Friends, examine yourselves to see if you're in the faith. Test yourself to know if Jesus is really in your heart.

I'll close this chapter with a threefold test to determine if a person is a false teacher. First, determine if their message is biblical. Does their message match the Word of God, and does it line up with the entire counsel of God? Second, look at their lifestyle. Their lifestyle should model Christ-like qualities. Behavior is always preceded by doctrine. When a person's doctrine is right, he or she will behave correctly. Third, look at their followers. Here's an interesting quote I heard recently: "Lost sheep will always follow a lost shepherd." When you see a teacher whose flock seems spiritually lost, wandering through life, easily misled, remember that lost sheep will always follow a lost shepherd. Look at the followers of this man's ministry or this woman's ministry. Do they have

152

a heart for godliness? Do they have a heart for holiness? Because we know that godly leaders will never claim to be satisfied with ungodly converts.

John MacArthur says it this way: "Christ-honoring, Scripture-loving preachers and teachers will produce Christ-honoring, Scripture-loving people. But charlatans will produce only mirror images of themselves."[24]

My prayer is that you will have the spiritual discernment to tell the difference.

chapter 13

Four Skills of a Disciple-Maker

2 TIMOTHY 3:10-17

W e need four critical skills in order to accomplish our mission of being effective disciple-makers. Paul describes these skills in 2 Timothy 3:10–17. He writes:

> 10 You, however, have followed my teaching, my conduct, my aim in life, my faith, my patience, my love, my steadfastness, 11 my persecutions and sufferings that happened to me at Antioch, at Iconium, and at Lystra—which persecutions I endured; yet from them all the Lord rescued me. 12 Indeed, all who desire to live a godly life in Christ Jesus will be persecuted, 13 while evil people and impostors will go on from bad to worse, deceiving and being deceived. 14 But as for you, continue in what you have learned and have firmly believed, knowing from whom you learned it

15 and how from childhood you have been acquainted with the sacred writings, which are able to make you wise for salvation through faith in Christ Jesus. 16 All Scripture is breathed out by God and profitable for teaching, for reproof, for correction, and for training in righteousness, 17 that the man of God may be competent, equipped for every good work.

Follow a Christlike Example

As believers and teachers of the Word, you and I need to devote ourselves to being competent and fully equipped for every good work, just like Timothy. The first way we can do this is by *following a Christlike example.*

In verse 10, Paul writes to Timothy, "You, however, have followed my teaching." He contrasts Timothy's faithful living with the negative way that false teachers live, as he describes in 2 Timothy 3:1–9. In essence, Paul is saying, "They may live in a sinful way, but, Timothy, I want you to live this way instead: follow my teaching and my conduct." Then Paul outlines how he has lived his life since he became a believer in Christ.

The word *follow* in verse 10 is the same word used to describe the way a surgeon examines a patient or the way a detective investigates a crime. Paul knows that Timothy is not just investigating or examining his life at the moment, but has been doing so for years. He has seen the way Paul lived and listened closely to the things Paul taught. Because of this, he understood that Paul was a man of God, not only in word, but also in deed. Paul realized that Timothy had watched his life so closely that Paul could send him in his place and Timothy would live out the same beliefs that Paul himself had lived out.

When we read verses 10 and 11, it almost sounds like Paul is boasting, doesn't it? After all, he seems to be drawing attention to his own commendable level of correct teaching, conduct, focus, faith, patience, love, steadfastness, and perseverance through persecution and suffering.

But in the Greek, all the words point to these two words: *patience* and *steadfastness*. Paul's point is actually that Timothy needs to remember these things so that he can persevere through persecution and trials. The same applies to us today.

Then Paul lists three specific cities in which he endured suffering. He could have picked any of the cities in which he worked and ministered. He could have picked Philippi. He could have picked Corinth, which was a city with plenty of spiritual and moral issues of its own. But Paul chose Antioch, Iconium, and Lystra, for a reason.

According to Acts chapters 13 and 14, the Jews in Antioch tried to hurt Paul, so he fled to Iconium. In Iconium, he was also attacked. Once again, the Jews tried to kill him. Then we find an interesting verse. Paul traveled to Lystra, which commentators believe that was Timothy's hometown.

I think he chose these three cities because his experiences there with Timothy have left a vivid impression in Timothy's mind. I believe Timothy probably replayed the event that I'm going to describe to you next over and over. Look what happens in the text.

Acts 14:19–20 says that the Jews in Lystra "stoned Paul and dragged him out of the city, supposing that he was dead. But when the disciples gathered about him, he rose up and entered the city, and on the next day he went on with Barnabas to Derbe." Now, that's quite a miracle. I believe that Paul really was dead. As a young man in his own city, Timothy witnessed people throwing stones and cracking the skull and the bones of Paul. Blood dripped from his head and body, and he was left for dead. The Jews literally dragged him out of the city and left him there. He lay lifeless on the ground.

Timothy and the disciples at that time probably gathered around him and mourned the death of their mentor. They probably had no idea what to do next or how their mission could continue. Then, all of a sudden, one of Paul's eyes popped open. Then the other eye opened. Then Paul, the way he always did, slowly got to his feet, dusted himself off, and said, "All right, boys, there'll be no funeral today. Let's go!"

That's how I imagine the scene. I love what verse 20 says: Paul "rose up and entered the city, and on the next day he went on with Barnabas to Derbe." Friends, Paul didn't take a sabbatical even after being dead. Even then he says, "This mission is too important for us to wait. Let's keep going."

What a vivid memory this must have created in Timothy's mind! This is his fearless leader; this is the apostle that he's following. Paul doesn't remind Timothy of this in order to brag about his faith, love, and patience; he does it to prove a point. He wants Timothy to know that even though he did everything right, he was still persecuted. He was the one who showed up for church every service, who was preaching from the pulpit. He didn't just go on mission trips; he organized them as well. He was the prayer coordinator, the banquet holder, and the outreach manager. And because of all the good deeds he did for Christ and the church, he was severely persecuted.

Have you ever noticed that in God's economy, good guys sometimes seem to finish last? That's because this world is not our home. The world is not friendly to the things and the people of God. But sometimes the enduring is the rescuing. When you are able to endure a difficult trial, that endurance may be your "rescuing" from God.

In fact, Paul was led to the Lord in part by witnessing the courage of a Christian man named Stephen who faced persecution and death for his faith. Do you remember this? Acts chapter 9 contains the story of Stephen being stoned. Paul was not only there watching this; he was watching the cloaks of the men who were throwing the rocks.

Paul heard Stephen's confession of faith, and in part because of Stephen's courage and his powerful testimony, Paul later came to Christ. How amazing that Timothy then saw Paul stoned and witnessed his bravery, helping Timothy commit his own life to Christ.

Friends, it's through the struggles of life that we learn to really reflect the Savior. That's why you need a godly mentor. You need someone in your life to whom you can look for guidance, like the apostle Paul. You need a person you can talk to, listen to, watch, and learn from.

I want to ask you, who are you hanging out with? You know, your friends will determine your future. In fact, I used to say this when I traveled and spoke at youth events. I told the youth, "Listen, if you want to know your future, take a photograph of your friends, because that picture will tell you where you're going." If you don't like where you're going, you need to change who you spend time with.

Persevere through Difficulty

Paul also teaches that we need to *persevere through difficulty.* This is something you can write down and take to the bank!

Expect Persecution

All who desire to live a godly life in Christ Jesus will suffer persecution. That word *all* can be translated better as "anybody, everybody, or anyone." Anyone who desires to serve the Lord faithfully will suffer persecution. We should anticipate it and expect it. Friends, we will always experience persecution in the world, because the world is hostile toward God. Jesus taught in Matthew 5:11, "Blessed are you when others revile you and persecute you and utter all kinds of evil against you falsely on my account." Jesus is saying, "Count it all joy when people talk badly about you for My name's sake." Notice that He says "when" and not "if."

Paul told the church at Thessalonica in 1 Thessalonians 3:4, "For when we were with you, we kept telling you beforehand that we were to suffer affliction, just as it has come to pass, and just as you know." Suffering and persecution are a part of the Christian life.

I understand that getting a grip on this truth is very challenging for us. When I look at the American church, I don't see a lot of suffering in the same way that Paul experienced suffering in the first century. In fact, as we were driving to church one day recently, I asked my wife, "Do you think we suffer?" She told me that she doesn't think that we suffer, at least not in the way that many other people do.

There's a connection in the text between standing up for the Lord and suffering. Paul is saying this: "When you stand up for the Lord and preach the gospel faithfully and openly, your level of suffering will increase." Now here's the flip side. When you do *not* stand up for the Lord and you cower down in the face of suffering, you probably will not experience much persecution in the world.

My prayer is that God will continue to raise up leaders in this church and around the country who will not cower down in the face of persecution. I hope that when you're asked questions about God at home, at work, or anywhere else, that you will confidently share the gospel with this attitude: "I am not about to cower down. I expect persecution, I anticipate persecution, and if I'm not being persecuted, then maybe I'm not doing or saying what God wants me to."

Understand Imposters

Not only should we expect persecution, we must *understand imposters*. Paul is referring back to the group of men he talked about in verses 1 through 9. In chapter 3, verse 6 he talks about false teachers, and in chapter 3, verse 8, he mentions Jannes and Jambres. I believe that this passage should be translated to read: "evil people who are imposters." That's the flow of the text in the Greek.

The Greek word *imposter* means "one who howls or wails." This is because the magicians and sorcerers had a habit of howling or wailing when they engaged in their rituals of worshiping false gods. So in the Greek we find the suggestion that if a person wailed and howled during a church service, he or she was a false teacher or an imposter in the church.

We don't need to evangelize just outside the church; we also have a mission field in the church. If evil men or imposters are in the church, then we need not focus our efforts only outside of the church; we need to focus our efforts inside the church as well. Another church member, a family member, or friend of yours could in fact be lost, having the appearance of godliness, but denying its power.

You might be thinking, "I know I need to follow a godly example, and I know that I need to persevere in difficulty, but how do I do that?"

Abide in the Word

Paul's third point is that we need to abide in the Word, because the teaching of these imposters will "go on from bad to worse." That's actually a play on words in the Greek. Paul literally says, "They will descend." Sin always takes you farther down than you want to go.

How do you avoid this type of downward spiral? Verses 14 and 15 tell us: "But as for you, continue in what you have learned and have firmly believed, knowing from whom you learned it and how from your childhood you have been acquainted with the sacred writings." That word *continue* means "to abide." Jesus says in John 15:4–5, "Abide in me, and I in you. As the branch cannot bear fruit by itself, unless it abides in the vine, neither can you, unless you abide in me. I am the vine; you are the branches. Whoever abides in me and I in him, he it is that bears much fruit, for apart from me you can do nothing."

Abide means to remain, to continue walking on the path of truth.

The Importance of Discipleship

As part of abiding in Christ, Paul gives Timothy two pointers. First, Paul reminds him of *the importance of discipleship*. He says basically, "Timothy, the reason you are who you are is because of two godly women: your grandmother, Lois, and your mother, Eunice. Because these two women invested in your life, you have become the man that you were created to be in God." The spiritual legacy of Timothy's grandmother and mother—two women—produced one godly man.

What kind of spiritual legacy are you leaving in your home? Do you live in a way that shows your spouse and children that God is paramount? Do you live with scripture as your divine authority? Do you teach your family that God and His Word are sufficient for all things? Or do you just casually go through life? Friends, we live in a secular world. If we don't intentionally teach our children about God, the world will teach them about other things.

My friend Collin and I were eating at a restaurant recently, and we were talking to the owner of the restaurant. I've invited this restaurant owner to church numerous times. Finally, I decided to invite him again. I asked him, "Why don't you come to church?"

He said, "Robby, I'll be frank with you. I work all week. I run the restaurant from Monday through Saturday. I hardly have any time with my kids, so when I'm off on Sunday, we spend the day together."

I said, "Oh, okay. I can appreciate that."

He said, "But do you know what's baffling to me? My kids are now nine and eleven, and a few days ago, I said something about David and Goliath." He paused. "My son looked at me and asked, 'David and Goliath? Who are you talking about, Dad?'"

He went on, "I was raised in a Christian home, but now, because I'm not influencing my kids, they don't know any of the stories of the Old Testament or the New Testament."

He told me this as Collin and I were signing the bill. I'll never forget it. He said, "Robby, I don't want to force my kids to believe in God. I don't want to force them to pray. I don't want to force them to believe in something they don't want to believe in."

Without hesitation, I looked straight at him and said, "Brother, you'd better start forcing them to believe in something, because the world has already started. Every day, the world is teaching them that sexual immorality is good. The world is teaching them that sin is cool. The world is teaching them that greed and money and success and a bigger house and a bigger car and a better job are the way to go. If you don't start teaching your kids now, you're going to be in a world of trouble. Start now, or it will be too late."

The Impact of Scripture

We've seen what Paul says about the importance of discipline. Second, Paul tells us that we must remember and teach others about the impact of scripture. He reminds us that "the sacred writings" are "able to make you wise for salvation through faith in Christ Jesus." We know he is talking about the Old and New Testament scriptures, but did you know that the Old Testament alone is sufficient for leading someone to faith in Jesus Christ?

I once attended a messianic conference with the theme "The Jew-ishness of Jesus." My roommate was a messianic Jewish rabbi. He was a Jewish man who had chosen to trust in Jesus as the Messiah for his salva-tion. He asked me this question one night. I'll never forget it. He asked, "How do you lead someone to Christ? Where do you start?"

I said, "I start in the book of Romans." Then I asked him, "Where do you start?"

He said, "I start in the book of Genesis."

He was right; the message of God's salvation begins at the begin-ning of time. That's where Jesus started as he talked to the two men on the road to Emmaus? Those two men were walking and discussing the events surrounding the crucifixion of Jesus. Jesus met them and said, "Let me show you who Jesus is from the Old Testament." He brought them through the entire Old Testament and showed them how it all pointed to Himself as the Messiah. Then He disappeared. Only after that did their hearts burn and sigh with understanding because they finally realized that they had just met Jesus, the Christ, the Son of God.

We live in a world today where people love to say, "All roads lead to God." People often tell me, "I believe all roads lead to heaven." I'm sorry, but that's just not true, friends. Logically as well as biblically, it *can't* be true. Acts 4:12 says, "There is no other name under heaven given among men by which we must be saved." The Bible is the only book that reveals God's plan of salvation for His people. It is the book of His revelation, and it points people to heaven by faith in Christ alone. Jesus is the Way. There is no other.

The entire Bible points to Christ. The Old Testament foretells the coming of Jesus, the Messiah; the New Testament describes Jesus' life on earth; and the book of Revelation talks about His return (the second coming of Christ). It's all about Jesus.

Respond to the Word

When we read scripture, it's important for us to *respond to the Word.* Paul finishes the text with a reminder about the power of scripture. He reminds Timothy of scripture's divine origin and divine purpose.

The Divine Origin of Scripture

In verse 16, Paul writes, "All scripture is breathed out by God." The New International Version says, "God-breathed." The New Living Translation and New American Standard say, "All Scripture is inspired by God." This term is a combination of the two Greek words *theos,* which means God, and *pneu,* which means breath. Paul puts those two words together to describe the character and the quality of scripture. He says it's God-breathed. The word *pneu* is where we get our words *pneumatic,* as in pneumatic drill or pneumatic tires, and *pneumonia.* It's the word for breath. He's saying that scripture is God-breathed, God-driven, and God-inspired. When God breathed life into the scriptures, they took on the divine quality and the divine characteristic of the essence of who He is. When you and I get into the Word, it's like spending time with God Himself. That's why Jesus says in John 1:1, "In the beginning was the Word, and the Word was with God, and the Word was God." Then in verse 14, John says, "And the Word became flesh." Jesus was the walking Word.

The Baptist Faith and Message says it this way: "The Holy Bible was written by men divinely inspired and is God's revelation of Himself to man."[25]

Imagine a person, after reading a book, saying, "I don't really like the book very much. I don't really get it." But then imagine he gets to know the author of the book. As he begins to know the author more intimately, he falls in love with the content of the book, and that changes the way he reads the book. He starts to love the book. He gets inspired by the book. The same thing goes for the Bible. When you fall in love with the author of the Book, the Book comes to life. You'll be inspired by the Book. You'll be amazed by the Book. The Book will transform your life.

The Divine Purpose of Scripture

Next, Paul reminds Timothy that while he knows that scripture originate from God, he must also look at its divine purpose. He names four specific elements of the purpose.

The word *teaching* that Paul uses in verse 10 is the word for *doctrine*. Did you know that Paul wrote most, if not all, of his letters with this frame of reference? He wrote four books about doctrine: Romans, Ephesians, and 1 and 2 Thessalonians. He wrote Romans about the doctrine of the cross. He wrote Ephesians about the doctrine of the church. He wrote 1 and 2 Thessalonians about the doctrine of the second coming of Christ.

Then he uses the word *reproof*. It's the idea of correcting the errors of false teaching. He wrote three books about this. In 1 Corinthians, he rebuked the immorality in the church. In 2 Corinthians, he rebuked the church at Corinth regarding the need for church discipline. And in the third book, Philippians, he rebuked the Philippian Christians about losing their focus on Christ. They were falling away from the church and straying from the truth.

The third term Paul uses is *correction*. It means "to restore to an upright position or action." It also means "to bring someone back to the path they have strayed from." This is the only time this specific term is used in the New Testament. There are two books that Paul uses to correct incorrect doctrinal beliefs: the book of Galatians (the people had shifted to a different gospel); and the book of Colossians (the people were not able to understand the lordship of Christ).

Finally, Paul refers to *training*. This word *training* is the word for *discipline*. It means "to take a child and to train him or disciple her in order to bring her back to the Lord." Paul says that Timothy needs to train himself in order to be equipped for the work of the ministry. As we mentioned in a previous chapter, it's the idea of an athlete training. It's the idea of a soldier preparing to go to war. It's the idea of a farmer diligently planting and harvesting crops. Paul says that when you get into the Word, the Word will train you and equip you.

Friends, the Word was supreme in Timothy's life. The Word was supreme in Paul's life. I want to ask you, is the Word supreme in your life? Do you love the Word?

I have a suspicion that many of us used to have a passion for the Word. When we were new believers, we used to love spending time in the Word. Think back to that time. when You would wake up and begin reading the Word. You would memorize and quote the Word. You would read the Word before going to bed. Sadly, as life progresses and as the Christian life moves on, we begin to take the Word for granted, and we don't read it like we used to. We don't study it like we used to. We don't labor over it like we used to.

Friends, do you know what the beauty and the purpose of reading the Word is? It's that Greek word *competence*—"so that the man of God may be competent." That doesn't mean just to know things; it means "to gain the wisdom to fulfill your divine purpose in life."

Paul is teaching us that if we are immature in the Word, we will never be all that God created us to be, period. I've never met an immature believer in the Word that God used to the fullest capacity that he or she could be used. In order to do all and be all you can be, you must immerse yourself in the Word.

I have prayed for God to continue to grant me a passion for the Word, because it doesn't always come naturally. You don't always wake up with a burning desire to get into the Word, because the flesh and the devil and the world are pitted against you. So you need to pray, "God, give me a passion for the Word."

I love the Word. I labor over the Word. I want to learn the Word. The Bible says that God's Word is living and active, sharper than any two-edged sword, piercing even to the division of soul and spirit, joint and marrow, discerning the thoughts and the intentions of a person's heart. God also says that His Word will never come back void. It will always accomplish the purpose it was meant to accomplish.

People ask me all the time, "Robby, how did you get to where you are so quickly?" Or, they'll say, "How did the Lord use you? There's nothing special about you."

I tell them, "You're right; there's nothing special about me. My ministry is not due to any talent or speaking ability on my part."

If someone were to ask me, "Why do you think the Lord has been able to use you in this capacity?" I would simply say, "I knew from day one when I became a believer that I had to make the Word the supreme authority in my life." I knew this because my mentors, David Platt and Tim LaFleur, taught me this and invested in my life. I knew that I needed to get in the Word until the Word got into me. I needed to love the Word and spend time in the Word and memorize the Word and saturate myself with the Word and meditate on the Word. My entire life is simply a product of God's Word.

I believe the reason we see so many immature, undisciplined disciples in the church and in the world is because they are not immersing themselves in the Word of God. Friends, an effective disciple-maker must be consistently in the Word. Do all you can to cultivate a passionate love for the scriptures.

chapter 14

Communicating God's Truth
No Matter the Circumstances

2 TIMOTHY 4:1-5

It's no surprise that the Christian church of the Lord Jesus Christ is struggling in some ways. In fact, I would say that we've found our-selves in quite a mess. We live in a world that is hostile to the biblical message of salvation through Christ alone. In addition, we face a lot of false teaching, both inside and outside of the church. In this chapter, I want to provide you with a message and a mission to help you combat false teaching and be equipped to share God's Word, no matter the cir-cumstances.

Let's read what Paul writes to Timothy in 2 Timothy 4:1–5:

1 I charge you in the presence of God and of Christ Jesus, who is to judge the living and the dead, and by his appearing and his kingdom: 2 preach the word; be ready in season and out of season;

reprove, rebuke, and exhort, with complete patience and teaching. 3 For the time is coming when people will not endure sound teaching, but having itching ears they will accumulate for themselves teachers to suit their own passions, 4 and will turn away from listening to the truth and wander off into myths. 5 As for you, always be sober-minded, endure suffering, do the work of an evangelist, fulfill your ministry.

What Is the Mandate?

The mandate that Paul gives Timothy in this passage is to *preach the Word*. He exhorts him, "I charge you ... to preach the Word." Although Paul is writing to Timothy here, we can apply this mandate to the life of every Christian. We are all in ministry together. One of the problems in the denomination I was raised in as a child is that the priest was the head of the church and he kept himself very separate from (and "spiritually superior to") the laity. The lay people thought that all of the spiritual responsibility should fall on the priest. In fact, they didn't think that they *could* do any of the duties of the priest, even if they had wanted to.

But we know from 1 Peter 2:9 that we're a royal priesthood. We're all called to do the work of the ministry. Paul makes a pretty powerful charge in verse 1, saying, "I charge you in the presence of God and of Christ Jesus, who is to judge the living and the dead, and by his appearing and his kingdom."

In the last days, two kinds of judgments will happen. The first is the judgment of believers after the rapture. According to 1 Corinthians 3:12, all believers will be judged based on the works and service we did for the Lord. Believers will *not* be judged on what we did to get into heaven, because we know that we are saved by grace through faith in Jesus Christ alone. Salvation is not something that we can earn; it is a gift from God. While we know that it true, we also know that all believers will be judged after the rapture. Secondly, there will be the Great White Throne Judgment described in Revelation chapter 20. This will be the final judgment of unbelievers.

Why does Paul give Timothy such a solemn and serious charge? Why does he evoke the names of Christ and God? And why does he refer to the fact that Jesus Christ will judge the living and the dead? I believe he does these things for one reason: to remind us that Jesus is the judge and we will be responsible to Him if we do not share the gospel.

You can fool me all you want, but the real question is, can you fool God? The Lord knows your heart, and He will be the ultimate judge. As pastors, teachers, church leaders, and believers in general, we have to remember that you and I are not accountable just to a church congregation; we're not accountable just to a board of elders or to the deacon body; we're not accountable just to our denomination. We are solemnly charged by God and Christ Jesus that one day, when all the dust has settled, we will walk into eternity and stand face to face with the living God. We will have to give an account to Him for every word we've said, every thought we had, and every deed we did. What a great responsibility that we have been given by the Lord!

What Is the Message?

While our mandate is to preach, our message is *the Word of God*. The Greek term for *preach* means "to herald," "to announce," or "to bring good news to people." The good news is God's Word. God has used His Word to accomplish His plans from the beginning of time. I don't know if you realize this, but God started all the way back in Genesis chapter 1 when He said, "Let there be light."

The Word of the Lord also came to Hosea, to Joel, to Amos, to Micah, to Zephaniah, to Haggai, to Zechariah, and to Jonah. Jonah was commissioned by God to go to Nineveh and preach the Word. Jesus says in Matthew 12:41 that the people of Nineveh "repented at the preaching of Jonah."

But the Word doesn't end in the Old Testament; the New Testament continues with the proclamation of God's truth. Jesus Christ was the embodiment of the Word of God. Ephesians 1:13 says, "In him you also, when you heard the word of truth, the gospel of your salvation, and believed in him, were sealed with the promised Holy Spirit."

First Peter 1:23–25 says, "Since you have been born again, not of perishable seed but of imperishable, through the living and enduring word of God; for . . . 'The grass withers, and the flower falls, but the word of the Lord remains forever.'"

How does the Bible end? John writes in Revelation 20:4, "Then I saw thrones, and seated on them were those to whom the authority to judge was committed. Also I saw the souls of those who had been beheaded for the testimony of Jesus and for the word of God."

Friends, we need to expect pastors and preachers to stand up at the sacred pulpit of God and not simply preach their own personal opinions or tell cool stories or share great ideas apart from the Word. We should expect to hear pastors preaching the Word of God.

Here is what Haddon Robinson, the great expositor, says: "Not all passion and pleading from the pulpit, however, has divine authority. While a preacher must herald, he must herald the Word."[26]

Why, exactly, do we need to preach the Word? Paul provides the reasoning and the formula in Romans 10:13–17:

> For "everyone who calls on the name of the Lord will be saved."
>
> How then will they call upon him in whom they have not believed? And how are they to believe in him of whom they have never heard? And how are they to hear without someone preaching? And how are they to preach unless they are sent? As it is written, "How beautiful are the feet of those who preach the good news!" . . . So faith comes from hearing, and hearing through the word of Christ.

This is a very different teaching from what was taught in the denomination I was raised in. I was raised in a denomination that didn't focus on the Word as the center of the service. The Eucharist (communion) was the focal point.

I do believe that observing the Lord's Supper is an important ordinance of the church, but it should not be the number-one focus. The

Eucharist, as it is called, is not going to save the souls of the lost. The Word is what saves us. Faith comes by hearing, and hearing by the Word of Christ. You need to hear the Word. You need to love the Word. You need to saturate your life with the Word.

Paul also reminds us that we need to "be ready in season and out of season." We should be ready messengers of the gospel. We should be urgent in our focus on the task to which we have been called. We should be eager to share the gospel at all times, in every situation. Consider the example of Jesus as he traveled by foot all the way through Samaria. He was exhausted after His long journey and sat down by a well to rest. His disciples have gone into town to buy food when He saw a woman at the well and recognized her need. He could have said to Himself, "I'm too tired right now to talk to this lady." But He was ready in season and out of season. He asked her for a drink and started a spiritual conversation with her. She admitted to her sinful past, and He shared with her that He is the living water. He met her at the point of her need, and as a result, she trusted in Him as the Messiah. Jesus was always ready. How about you?

1 Peter 3:15 says, "In your hearts honor Christ the Lord as holy, always being prepared to make a defense to anyone who asks you for a reason for the hope that is in you; yet do it with gentleness and respect."

Now, notice the next three commands in 2 Timothy. Two of the three are negative; one is positive. The first command is to *reprove*. It's the idea of convincing. It means to use scripture to reason with a person who is lost as you seek to lead him or her to Christ.

Next, we should *rebuke*. This is the act of reasoning with a person who knows the Lord, but has done a U-turn or strayed from the Lord. To rebuke is to convince this person of his sin and lead him back into fellowship with Christ. Regardless, both of these terms are negative.

Then Paul switches gears commands Timothy to *exhort*. The word *exhort* is the word for instruction or encouragement. The only way that I believe you can faithfully preach or instruct the Word is by carefully sharing God's truth through expository teaching. Friends, this is why it is so important for you to be in a church led by a pastor who faithfully and accurately preaches the Word of God.

Now, why does Paul finish by mentioning "complete patience"? If you've ever been involved in pastoral or church ministry, you know that it requires a heaping measure of patience and grace. Helping people grow spiritually takes time, right? Many people don't develop as fast as you would like them to. But Paul says in essence, "Timothy, don't get nervous. People will develop, but it will take time, so be patient. Wait upon the Lord."

What Is the Mess?

Now, let me show you the mess we are in. What Paul describes starting in verse 3 is a downward spiral. It's a slippery slope. You don't just wake up one day and discover that you've believed a myth. It's a gradual process of being led astray from the truth.

Here's how the process works. First of all, you will turn aside and *avoid sound teaching*. You begin to say, "You know, I'm not sure I like biblical preaching." You begin to pick and choose the parts of the Bible you want to study and the parts of the Bible that you don't want to study. You begin to think, "I don't want to hear confrontational preaching. I prefer 'feel good' messages. I want to hear about how I can have my best life now.".

Next, you start following and *accumulating false teachers*. You don't just wake up one day and begin to listen to false teachers. I have a close friend back home who listens to some of the false teachers of the health, wealth, and prosperity gospel. He likes to hear the message that says, "If you come to Jesus, He'll give you every material thing you've ever wanted." This man started down this path by turning away and avoiding sound teaching.

Then you begin to *reject biblical truth*. Paul mentions people with "itching ears. Many people in our culture don't want to hear sound teaching; they simply want the preacher to tickle their ears with "feel good" messages. We love to hear good things. We love to hear sermons about heaven and eternity. We love to hear sermons about how God is out to bless us, right. We love those messages.

But not many of us want to hear how sinful we are. Not many of us want to hear that there's a real hell and that millions of real people will go there for eternity. We don't want to hear about God's justice or His wrath against sin. We don't like to hear about the evil in the world. But if I'm going to be a faithful, biblical preacher of the Word, I have to preach the whole counsel of God.

There are preachers who have said on the record, and I quote, "I will not preach on sin. I will not preach on the cross. I will not preach negative sermons." Anyone who will not preach on those topics is not preaching the scriptures. Let me ask you: do you have the discernment to know false teaching when you hear it? Can you spot a fake? Could you spot *yourself* if you began to be led astray by false doctrine? I believe the reason church goers wander off into false teaching is that they don't know the Word well enough themselves. Kay Arthur, the founder of Precept Ministries and author of numerous inductive Bible studies, told me recently, "It's not just the church as a whole; it's individual people who need to know the Word better."

The truth is, many of us are spiritually illiterate when it comes to the Bible. As a result, we begin to avoid sound teaching, start listening to false teachers, and reject biblical truth. In the New International Version, Paul says such people "will not put up with sound doctrine." That word *doctrine* is the word for the whole counsel of God. We're called to believe and preach the whole counsel of God.

I have to warn you that when you preach, teach, or share the whole counsel of God, you run the risk of losing people from your congregation, your class, or your group. I know personally of a recent visitor to our church (a relative of a staff member) who said, "I'm not coming back. Your pastor preaches too hard. The sermons are too convicting. I'm not into confronting people. I want to focus on love and unity now in my later days. I want to hear about how good I am; I don't want to hear about sin and all of those other things."

Charles Haddon Spurgeon said, "Sermons should have real teaching in them and their doctrine should be solid, substantial, and abundant. We do not enter the pulpit to talk for talk's sake; we have instructions to convey the importance to the last doctrine and we cannot afford to utter pretty nothings."[27]

The problem begins with avoiding sound teaching. Then You begin to accumulate false teachers. You begin to reject biblical truth. And, finally, *you accept false teaching.* Basically, what happens is this: you "wander off into myths." That word *myths* is the word for fables; it's the word for fiction. *Mythos* is the Greek word; it's the opposite of *logos,* which is the term for the enduring Word of God.

Paul is saying that if you start believing *mythos,* you have wandered from the Word. Paul warns Timothy and Titus in every one of the pastoral Epistles to be sure to avoid wandering off into myths.

Walter Kaiser said, "It is no secret that Christ's church is not all in the best of health in many places of the world. She has been languishing because she has been fed as the current line has it—junk food. All kinds of artificial preservatives and all sorts of unnatural substitutes have been served up for her. As a result, theological and biblical malnutrition has afflicted the very generation that has taken such giant steps to make sure its physical health is not damaged by using foods or products that are harmful to the physical body."[28]

Many of us go to great lengths to keep our physical body from taking in junk food; yet, there are people sitting in church services on Sunday morning ever week ingesting spiritual junk food. How do we combat that? Well, consider where you are. People don't start accepting false teaching overnight; it starts gradually. They start throwing out small pieces of the Bible. "Oh, that doesn't apply to me. This doesn't matter to me. Oh, I like that, but I don't really want this. Thank goodness, the pastor says he's not going to preach about sin anymore. He's not going to talk about the cross anymore. He's only going to preach positive messages."

I'm reminded of a story about John Wesley. He was teaching a class late in his life, and one of his students asked him, "Mr. Wesley, what do you think about this passage? What does it mean?"

He looked at it and said, "I don't know what that passage means."

Surprised, his student responded, "What do you mean, you don't know what that passage means? Doesn't it bother you that you don't know?"

And John Wesley wisely responded, "Son, it's not the things in the Bible that I don't know that I have a problem with. It's the things in the Bible that I *do* know that I struggle with."

Friends, it's not all the things we don't know; it's the things we do know. Did you know that there is actually a trend right now for churches to replace their real, physical pastors with "virtual pastors"? Brother Don Lawrence preaches three times a week to an appreciative congregation at Life Baptist Church. Brother Don's sermons sell out every week. People tune in to him and watch him. They laugh at his jokes. They applaud him. They say "Amen" when he makes a good point. But here's the problem: *Brother Don is not real.* He's a virtual pastor on a screen.

Believe it or not, with a "virtual pastor," the church body gets to vote and determine the kind of pastor they want. There's a drop box and the church members fill out forms and say, "We want this kind of pastor. We want him to have this color of hair. We want him to have this color of eyes. We want him to wear polo shirts, not suits. We want him to wear this kind of shoes. We want him to preach this kind of sermon."

One of Brother Don's church members says, "We've never been happier in our lives. We finally have the pastor we have always wanted." Yes, but he isn't real.

Friends, when the people of God have too much input and influence over the man of God who preaches the Word of God by the power of God for the glory of God, we have missed the point. Whenever we say, "It's about me and what I want," we miss the point. We become the focal point, and we detract attention away from God and the message of His Word.

The great pastor George Whitefield said, "It is a poor sermon that gives no offense."[29] If a pastor's message doesn't ever give anyone offense or cause anyone to examine his or her heart, it might not be biblical proclamation. In the long run, that sermon doesn't benefit the hearer or the preacher.

What Is the Mission?

What is the mission we need to follow through with? Paul states it very simply in four points: *stay sober, endure suffering, spread the gospel,* and *finish strong.* Essentially, he says, "Timothy, be sober-minded. Stay free of intoxicants or anything else that will mislead you from the truth. Be level-headed. Be balanced in your ministry. Endure suffering. Spread the gospel, Timothy. Share the message of redemption, and finish strong. Fight the good fight."

At this point, you might think about writing off the responsibility of being an evangelist. You might say, "Well, Pastor, I'm just not gifted as an evangelist. Sorry. That's someone else's job description." But the beautiful thing about this passage is that Paul gets rid of that excuse. He reminds Timothy, "I'm not calling you to the *office* of an evangelist; I'm calling you to do the *work* of an evangelist. I know you're called to pastor and to preach, but I also want to charge you to go into the world and share the redemption message. Tell people that Jesus Christ came to the earth, died on the cross, rose from the dead, and ascended into heaven so that you and I can have peace with God and be indwelt by the Holy Spirit. Timothy, you need to go and give people that message."

How about you? Are you doing the work of an evangelist? Are you telling your family members, friends, colleagues, and neighbors about Christ? Have you *ever* talked to one of your neighbors about Jesus? Have you even asked a question to try to determine the spiritual nature of your neighbor? Paul basically says, "Timothy, you'd better get to know your neighborhood and the people in your community. Do the work of an evangelist."

Each of us has been called to some type of ministry. You've been called to fulfill a divine purpose. You have a network of people within your sphere of influence who need to hear the gospel and be saved. And if you don't tell them, then who will?

chapter 15

Growing in Passion
for Christ-like Living

2 TIMOTHY 4:6-8

A re you living a life with no regrets? As we look at the apostle Paul's departing remarks to his young disciple Timothy, we see that he was able to say, "I have lived my life without remorse or regrets."

When you stop and think about it, this is a truly remarkable statement. Paul had no regrets whatsoever? He was able to say this because of his fierce passion to serve God and to live like Christ. Paul's identity was firmly rooted in Jesus. In fact, he even wrote in Philippians 1:21, "For to me to live is Christ, and to die is gain." That should be our passion and our motto too.

In 2 Timothy 4:6–8, Paul writes:

6 For I am already being poured out as a drink offering, and the time of my departure has come. 7 I have fought the good fight, I

have finished the race, I have kept the faith. 8 Henceforth there is laid up for me the crown of righteousness, which the Lord, the righteous judge, will award to me on that Day, and not only to me but also to all who have loved his appearing.

I want to identify three aspects of Paul's life that will motivate us to live a life with no regrets. By following these three steps, we also will be empowered to grow in our passion for Christlike living.

A Sacrificial Life Devoted to Christ

First, Paul lived *a sacrificial life devoted to Christ.* Now, we have to understand the context of this letter. Paul is alone in a dark, dreary, wet Roman dungeon. He is carefully penning the very last words that he will ever write to his young disciple Timothy. Up to this point, he has had a preliminary hearing. He will soon appear before Nero, who will pronounce the judgment upon him that will echo in his mind, but also in the ears of all the hearers there: "execution." Paul knows that his death is imminent.

Poured Out His Life

Because Paul realizes that his earthly life is about to draw to a close, he says in paraphrase, "My life has been poured out. I am on the altar, like a sacrificial offering unto the Lord." The translation of the word used for *poured out* is the word for the libation, or drink, offering. In the Old Testament, the drink offering was a type of sacrificial offering that the priest offered to the Lord. The priest took a vessel of wine and poured it out on the altar as a sacrifice to the Lord. Paul is saying, "My life is likened to a sacrifice."

We already know that Paul's life was a sacrifice to the Lord, but isn't it interesting that he also says that his death will be a sacrifice to the Lord? Many commentators believe that he uses this terminology because Paul knows that, as a Roman citizen, he will not be crucified.

He must have realized that he will be positioned on the chopping block and the sword of a Roman executioner will come down on his neck. His lifeblood will be spilled and physically poured out as an offering to the Lord.

I want to ask you today, is your life a sacrifice to the Lord? Are you living a life that is poured out to God? Are you sold out for Christ like Paul was, willing to live for Him and die for Him?

To be honest, a lot of us would have to say, "Well, I really don't like to talk about sacrifice." Why? Sacrifice means pain. But sacrifice in the Old and New Testaments did not necessarily have as much to do with pain as it had to do with the importance of the offering. In the Old Testament, a blood sacrifice was valuable to the Lord. That's why Paul says in Romans 12:1, "I appeal to you therefore, brothers, by the mercies of God, to present your bodies as a living sacrifice, holy and acceptable to God." The greatest sacrifice you can give to the Lord is yourself.

Prepared for His Departure

Second, Paul says in essence, "*I've prepared myself for departure.*" He felt confident that he completed the work that the Lord called him to do. So he tells Timoth, "I'm ready to check out. I've lived my life for the Lord."

According to Bible scholar William Barclay, the word *departure* in Greek actually can have four different meanings. First, it means "to untie a tent" or remove the rope from a stake in the ground around the tent. The second meaning is "to unyoke an ox in the field after plowing." The third is "to loosen the bonds or the handcuffs off the hands of an individual." And the fourth meaning is "releasing the mooring of a ship so it can head out to sea."

The fourth visual picture is the illustration that Paul is using here. He has prepared himself for the journey into eternity, and he is ready to untie the rope and let his ship head out to sea. He has poured out his life as a sacrifice for the Lord, and now it's time for him to depart.

Friends, did you know that being with Christ for eternity will be far better than anything you could ever experience in this world? Enjoying perfect communion with your Creator will be greater than even the best experiences in this life.

A Faithful Life Committed to Christ

Paul did not live for temporal things; his mind was focused on eternity. He realized that he had been placed on earth for only a short time. His desire was to be faithful to the Lord; to be focused on the Lord; and to be sacrificial in offering up his life to the Lord. He lived a faithful life, completely committed to Christ.

Paul summarizes his life's work in three verbs in verse 7. He *competed*; he *completed*; and he *guarded the gospel*. These three verbs appear in the perfect tense. If you study Greek grammar textbooks, they tell you that a succession of three consecutive perfect verbs indicates that the actions happened in the past, but they have present implications. In essence, Paul is saying, "I did these actions throughout my ministry, and not only do they have present implications, but they will continue to be done for all of eternity."

Paul competed by fighting the good fight. The word *fought* is interesting; it's the Greek term *agonizomai*. *Agonizomai* is where we get the English word *agony*. Jesus uses this word in Luke 13:24 when he says, "Strive [agonize, fight, work] to enter through the narrow door."

Paul means, "My life as a Christian was a life of agonizing for the sake of the gospel. My life was a life of enduring. My life was a life of persevering through suffering."

One commentator says, "Paul fought against Satan, he fought against principalities and powers, the world rules of this darkness and the heavenlies, against Jewish and pagan vices and violence. Paul fought against Judaism among the Galatians. He fought against fanaticism among the Thessalonians. He fought against contention and fornication and litigation among the Corinthians. He fought against incipient Gnosticism among Ephesians and Colossians; against fights without and fears within the church and last by not least; he fought against the law of sin and he fought against death operating within his own heart."[30]

As a believer in the Lord Jesus Christ, we fight a constant fight against sin, the devil, flesh, laziness, and ourselves. That's why Paul says that the Christian life is a life of competing, and it's also a life of completing. He says, "I have finished the race." This word for finished, *teleos,* is the same root word used in the Greek translation when Jesus is on the cross and says, "It is finished." It means "paid in full. Done. Completed."

Paul means, "God gave me a course to run, and I ran it well." He makes a connection here, stating that every Christian has been given a course to run. Hebrews 12:1 says, "Therefore, since we're surrounded by so great a cloud of witnesses, let us also lay aside every weight, and sin which clings so closely, and let us run with endurance the race that is set before us."

The writer of Hebrews tells us that two enemies will get in the way of our success in completing the course: sin and weight. It's intriguing that he separates sin from weight. We all know that sin will hinder us from running the race for the Lord, but what about this word *weight*? Weight in and of itself may not be a bad thing; in fact, it could be something good. But if it gets in the way of your ability to run for the Lord, it's a hindrance to the race.

Television is a great example of a weight that could hinder us in running the race. We all love watching TV, right? Watching television in and of itself is not morally wrong, but if it gets into the way of your spending time with the Lord and hearing from Him, or if it keeps you from spending quality time with your family, it could be a weight that hinders you in the Christian race. What about the Internet? We love surfing the net. We love using our laptops, cell phones, iPhones, and iPads. Lots of us love texting too. Our interests and hobbies can easily become an addiction. They may be positive in and of themselves, but if they prevent us from running the Christian race well, Paul says that they are hindering us. Paul says, "I didn't let anything get in my way or keep me from completing the race that God gave me to run."

You see, it's one thing to start off well in a race; it's quite another thing to finish well. Starting a marathon is simple; the challenge is actually being able to cross the finish line after successfully running more than twenty-six miles!

Some of you who are reading this may be close to reaching the finish line of your life. I just want to ask you, are you running with the same spiritual intensity that you started with many years ago? You started well right out of the blocks, but are you still running the race with joy and endurance? Are you still serving the Lord? Are you still spending time with the Lord?

It's encouraging to know that the course was not always easy for Paul. I think that he would say to us, "You know, I tried my best, but I'm not perfect. There were many times that I failed and faced setbacks in my ministry. I was persecuted in my ministry too—but the most important factor is that I stayed true to the Lord and completed the course that God gave me to run." The great British leader Winston Churchill said this: "Success is never final, failure is never fatal: it is the courage to continue that counts."[31]

How are you running the race? Are you staying on course? Are you on pace to finish well? I hope you are.

Paul says, I've completed, I've competed, and, third, I have guarded the gospel. "I have kept the faith." How do you guard the gospel? How do you keep the faith? How do you keep God's commandments? Paul gives us a clue in Ephesians 4:3 when he tells us to be "eager to maintain the unity of the Spirit in the bond of peace."

We might think that the best way to guard something is to put it in a safe deposit box and lock it up. But we know from 2 Timothy that Paul has a different understanding of guarding. He says that to guard the gospel is to give it away. Look at what he writes in 2 Timothy 1:14: "By the Holy Spirit who dwells in us, guard the good deposit entrusted to you." Paul guarded the gospel by entrusting it to Timothy and instructing him to do the same.

The problem that often keeps us from guarding the gospel is because we don't cherish the faith. In order for us to really appreciate something, we have to cherish it.

I once heard the story of a woman in France who was born blind and wasn't able to read. So she learned Braille, and someone gave her a copy of the Gospel of Mark in Braille. She had read through the Gospel of Mark with her fingers so many times that her fingers developed calluses and she wasn't able to read anymore. She had a doctor remove the top layer of skin on her fingers, thinking that the nerve endings would be more sensitive and then she would be able to feel and read again. But she was disappointed to find that this procedure made it even worse. She picked the Bible up to say farewell to the book that had been a blessing to her, the sweet Word of her heavenly Father. She brought the cherished book up to her lips, and she suddenly realized that she could feel the Braille with her lips. She could teach herself to read the scripture (literally) with her lips. And for the rest of her life, that's how she read her Bible.

Do you cherish the Word the way this woman did? Friends, in order for us to guard the gospel, we have to cherish the treasure. Paraphrased, Paul says, "I cherished the gospel. My life was poured out as an offering to the Lord. I competed, I completed, and I guarded the truth."

A Focused Life Rewarded by Christ

Finally, Paul says in essence, "*I have lived a focused life, and that has been rewarded by Christ.*" Paul almost seems to be celebrating at the end of the letter in verse 8 where he writes, "*Henceforth there is laid up for me the crown of righteousness*" (emphasis added). Can you feel his joy and anticipation? Paul is excited because he realizes that he will receive a great reward in heaven.

The term *laid up* is the word for "stored up." It means "to put in a safe place." Paul is saying, "I don't need to worry, because God has stored a treasure up for me. It's the crown of righteousness."

Now, this is not a crown made of precious metal adorned with jewels; it's actually the Greek term for a garland or wreath of flowers that are intertwined together and placed on an athlete's head. Paul would have known this custom from the Olympic Games. When a person won a race, the judges placed a wreath of honor on his head. That wreath was a prized possession. In fact, if you won the wreath, your entire town celebrated. Everyone wanted to receive this wreath.

Earlier, Paul tells the church at Corinth, "We do not run for a perishable wreath; we run for an imperishable one. There are people who are training to win a wreath that will quickly fade away, but we will receive a crown of righteousness."

Some commentators believe that we will receive a crown as a reward for our works, for our righteousness. Other commentators believe that the crown of life is the reward. I'm siding with the latter. I believe that the crown itself is life; that when you and I walk through the door of eternity, our reward for Christ's righteousness will be the crown of eternal life. What better reward could you and I receive than to live for eternity with Jesus Christ?

You may have heard of the TV show called *Flash Forward*. I was very intrigued by the premise of the show. In the show, everybody in the world blacks out for 137 seconds at the same time on the same day. During that 137 seconds, each person sees his or her own future. Some people see their future, and they are surprised by it. Some people see their future, and they're disappointed by it. And because each person has seen a glimpse of the future, he or she changes lifestyle habits in the present. For example, one man was being wheeled into the operating room for brain surgery, and the doctor said, "You're about to have brain surgery, and you don't even look bothered. How are you not anxious?"

The man answered, "Doc, you don't understand; I've already seen the future. I live."

I think that if Paul were here today, he would say, "My life is like that. I am so certain that I will live for eternity with the Lord that I am able to endure pain and suffering in the present."

Friends, we live and serve a God who has written the story's ending already. We know that we will be victorious. We win in the end. Because Paul knew the future victory, he was able to endure anything during the present. This is what allowed him to say, "For me to live is Christ, but if I die, it's gain because then I get to go and be with Jesus for eternity."

I think that's why Jesus, in John 14:1–3, gives His disciples a glimpse of what they will see and experience in glory. He wants to give them hope for the future. He says, "Let not your hearts be troubled. Believe in God; believe also in me. In my Father's house are many rooms. If it were not so, would I have told you that I go to prepare a place for you? And if I go and prepare a place for you, I will come again and will take you to myself, that where I am you may be also."

In other words, "Guys, listen to me. There is a wonderful place waiting for you. Go out and serve me faithfully. Compete, complete the work, and guard the gospel, because even if you die serving me, you will win. I've already conquered death and the grave."

Paul writes in Philippians 3:7–8, "But whatever gain I had, I counted as loss for the sake of Christ. Indeed, I count everything as loss because of the surpassing worth of knowing Christ Jesus my Lord. For his sake I have suffered the loss of all things and count them as rubbish, in order that I may gain Christ." The secret of Paul's ministry success was that he knew Christ so well that Jesus was enough for him. He trusted the sufficiency of the Lord.

I want to ask you today, is Jesus Christ enough for you? Do you trust Him as being completely sufficient for your every need? Is Jesus just an addition to your life, or *is He your life*? Because Paul is saying: "Jesus Christ is everything to me. He's not just an add-on to my life; He is my life. So for me to live is Christ and to die is gain."

I believe that if Paul had written hymns, he would have penned the words to this hymn. It actually began as a poem written in 1922 by a woman named Rhea Miller. Then George Beverly Shea set the words to music and made this hymn famous. These words sum up the life and attitudes of the apostle Paul:

I'd rather have Jesus than silver or gold;
I'd rather be His than riches untold;
I'd rather have Jesus than houses or lands,
I'd rather be led by His nail pierced hand.

I'd rather have Jesus than men's applause;
I'd rather be faithful to His dear cause;
I'd rather have Jesus than worldwide fame,
I'd rather be true to His holy name.

Than to be a king of a vast domain
Or be held in sin's dread sway,
I'd rather have Jesus than anything
This world affords today.[32]

Can you honestly say that you would rather have Jesus than anything else in this world? Can you honestly say, "Jesus is sufficient for me"? I believe the apostle Paul could say that.

chapter 16

Finishing Well

2 TIMOTHY 4:9-22

I want to ask you: what will you be remembered for? In our final chapter together, we're going to focus on how to finish well the work that God has called us to do. Let's take a look at Paul's parting remarks in 2 Timothy 4:9–22.

> 9 Do your best to come to me soon. 10 For Demas, in love with this present world, has deserted me and gone to Thessalonica. Crescens has gone to Galatia, Titus to Dalmatia. 11 Luke alone is with me. Get Mark and bring him with you, for he is very useful to me for ministry. 12 Tychicus I have sent to Ephesus. 13 When you come, bring the cloak that I left with Carpus at Troas, also the books, and above all the parchments. 14 Alexander the coppersmith did me great harm; the Lord will repay him according to his deeds. 15 Beware of him yourself, for he strongly opposed our message. 16 At my first defense no one came to stand by me, but

all deserted me. May it not be charged against them! 17 But the Lord stood by me and strengthened me, so that through me the message might be fully proclaimed and all the Gentiles might hear it. So I was rescued from the lion's mouth. 18 The Lord will rescue me from every evil deed and bring me safely into his heavenly kingdom. To him be the glory forever and ever. Amen.

19 Greet Prisca and Aquila, and the household of Onesiphorus. 20 Erastus remained at Corinth, and I left Trophimus, who was ill, at Miletus. 21 Do your best to come before winter. Eubulus sends greetings to you, as do Pudens and Linus and Claudia and all the brothers.

22 The Lord be with your spirit. Grace be with you.

Paul mentions quite a few different believers in this passage. We can assume that these men and women all professed Christ. We can assume that they all were baptized, that they all were a part of a ministry, and that they were all members of a church. We can assume that all of them, at some point, were important figures in the spread of the Christian movement in the first century. But some finished well, and others did not.

A Fellow Worker Who Fell Out of Fellowship

Paul describes six different types of people in this passage. The first one is this: *a fellow worker who fell out of fellowship*. Right out of the gate, Paul mentions a man who did not finish well. He writes, "For Demas, in love with this present world, has deserted me and gone to Thessalonica."

In order to understand this verse, you have to realize where the apostle Paul is. He is in prison, a short time away from being beheaded. He has been tried before the Roman Proconsul, and his sentence has been handed down—death. Now, he's all alone in a damp, dark dungeon. He feels that everyone has deserted him. It's in these tough times that he needs tough friends, but Paul has no one standing by his side. And Demas, a man Paul discipled and invested in, a friend about which Paul had said, "This man will never leave me or forsake me," has done that very thing: Demas has deserted Paul.

Let's find out more about Demas. Paul describes Demas as a fellow worker in the faith. In the book of Philemon, verse 24, Paul mentions "Demas, my fellow worker." If Paul had had a pastoral staff, Demas would have been one of his right-hand men.

Commentator William Barclay gives us interesting insight into this passage. Listen to what he says about Demas: "Maybe the years of following Christ have taken a toll on his life. They have made a way of taking away his ideals; of making a satisfaction with less and less, of lowering one's standards. There is no threat so dangerous and so insidious as the threat of years to a man's ideals."[33]

Not only do we have to watch out for evil men and false teachers; we also have to guard against becoming too comfortable in the Christian life. Over time, maybe Demas got so used to being a believer that he chose personal comfort over the cross. Or maybe he went after wealth or material possessions. We really don't know. All we know is that eventually, he deserted Paul.

Imagine Paul pacing in his cell with just a little light at the top, saying to himself, "How could Demas do this? Especially after all that we've been through together? I was there for him. He traveled with me. He helped me plant churches. I even wrote his name in several letters that I sent to the churches. How could he do this to me?" What a bitter pill for Paul to swallow.

You know, I have to be honest with you. The greatest disappointments in my life have been due not to the evil people in the world, but due to the people who were faithful to God at one time but then turned away from Him and turned away from me. Do you know anybody like that? I'm sure you've been there.

You've probably seen men and women who had so much potential for the Lord Jesus Christ, men and women who were faithful to God at one time, take a U-turn and began to live in sin or selfishness or immorality. They start following their own ways and their own ideals. Friends, listen to me. Don't turn your back on the Lord. Don't be like Demas. Remain faithful to the end.

Friends Supporting the Work of the Ministry

The second group of people we meet in the text is *a group of friends who supported the work of the ministry*. First, Paul mentions Titus: "Titus has gone to Dalmatia." Dalmatia was east of Rome and across the Adriatic Sea. Paul considered Titus to be a true son of the faith. He loved Titus.

Next, Paul mentions the physician and gospel writer Luke. Luke was a remarkable person who wrote both the Gospel of Luke and the book of Acts. As you read through the book of Acts, whenever you see Luke's statements saying "we traveled on this journey" or "we went to this area," you can assume that Luke is including himself in the group.

Luke accompanied Paul on his second missionary journey when he went to Philippi, and he traveled on to Troas. It appears that Luke accompanied Paul on his third missionary journey, too, meeting up with Paul in Philippi and then going on to Jerusalem. Luke was a man who was always there for Paul.

Let me focus on the one man mentioned in verse 10 that we know nothing about, and that is Crescens. Paul says that he went to Galatia. I had considered glossing over Crescens, but I decided I should stop and encourage you with this word, because it's amazing. As I studied the New Testament, looking for the name of Crescens, I came up empty. When I searched the concordances and the Bible dictionaries, I found only one reference to this man, and it appears here in this chapter and in this verse. I realized that Crescens was an unknown follower of Christ. All we know is that he decided to follow the calling of the Lord and go to Galatia, where a Christian church had been planted.

As I've said before, every word in the Bible is divinely inspired and is there for a reason. I believe there's a specific meaning behind Paul's mention of Crescens. Only in eternity with the Lord will we find out who he really is. Clearly, he was a faithful man who worked behind the scenes. There are many people like him. God knows them well; you may be one of them. You may be the one who will never stand on the pulpit or the stage. You may never receive the accolades and applause. But don't give up in serving the Lord, because God sees all that you do. It's not the generals and the leaders and the preachers and the teachers that make the church work; it's the quiet and faithful men and women who do all of the work behind the scenes. The backbone of the church is often made up of people we've never even heard of.

My challenge to you is this: if you are a Christian working behind the scenes, continue to serve faithfully, because God sees you and He appreciates you, and other people do too. That's the kind of man Crescens was.

A Deserting Partner Restored as a Friend

Third, we read about *a deserting partner restored as a friend*. I love this part. In 2 Timothy 4:11, Paul writes, "Luke alone is with me. Get Mark and bring him to me for he is useful to me for ministry." Why is this so important? At one time, Mark was a privileged man. If you think about it, Mark not only got to hang out with the apostles as a young kid, but Mark got to hang out with Jesus. He was a pretty important guy. What an honor to hang out with Jesus.

We also discover in Acts chapter 12 that Mark's mother's house was the house that Peter retreated to when he came back after being in prison. But something happened to Mark, according to Acts chapter 13. Paul, Barnabas, and Mark had embarked on a missionary journey (Paul's first journey), and right in the middle of the journey, for some unknown reason, Mark decided to check out and leave. He said, "Paul and Barnabas, I'm out of here. I have to go back home."

It appears that this desertion bothered Paul so much that Paul decided to cut Mark off and not work or travel with him anymore. On Paul's second missionary journey, Barnabas (who was Mark's cousin) approached Paul and said, "Hey! Let's bring Mark with us again on this mission trip. Let's go out and minister together with him."

Guess what Paul said? "No way. We're not bringing him. He deserted us once. I'm done with Mark." In fact, because of this disagreement,

Paul and Silas went one way, and Barnabas and Mark went another way. We don't find out what happened until Acts 15. In Acts chapter 15 and also in the book of Colossians, we realize that restoration has taken place between Paul and Mark. Aren't you glad that God paves the way for restoration in the Christian life?

The friendship and partnership between Paul and Mark is restored, and pay attention to what Paul says in Colossians 4:10: "Aristarchus my fellow prisoner greets you, and Mark the cousin of Barnabas." We don't know exactly how the relationship was mended, but we do know that Mark and Paul's friendship was restored. In fact, Mark was restored so completely that the apostle Peter refers to him in 1 Peter 5:13 as, "Mark, my son."

My point is that Mark, the former mission team dropout, became the gospel writer Mark. Mark's book is the action gospel that describes the servanthood of the Lord Jesus Christ. Aren't you glad that God gives us not just one or two chances, but multiple chances for service and restoration? Mark, the useless one, the deserter, became a useful servant. Because of that, we read his gospel in the Bible even today. Isn't that amazing?

If you are at a place in your life where you're thinking, "Pastor, I don't think God can use me. I'm just like Mark," you're wrong. Trust me. At the age of twenty-six, I had nothing. I had no job. I had no future. My family had just let me back in the house. I had thousands and thousands of dollars of debt. I was single. I had no direction. I had no friends. But I'm here to tell you, God began to use me. He helped me to make a major course correction on my life. I made the decision to change the way I was living, and because of that, God through His grace has restored me. He has been so gracious to me.

I want to encourage you today because it's never too late for God to use you. When I counsel people, I always tell them, "If there is life, there is hope." If you're still alive, God can still use you. He's still writing the story of your life. It's not too late to change the ending.

A Foe Destroying Ministry Plans

Fourth, we read about *a foe destroying ministry plans*. Paul mentions here that one man, Alexander the coppersmith, was a foe who tried to thwart his ministry plans. Paul writes, "Alexander the coppersmith did me great harm." Just imagine how terrible it would be if this was engraved on your tombstone: "this man (or woman) did great harm." Clearly, Alexander's actions were upsetting for Paul.

R. Kent Hughes says we don't understand what happened here, but Alexander may have been the accuser in Paul's trial or a witness in the prosecution that sent Paul to his death.[34] We do know this: Alexander was a very common name at that time. It is used in the New Testament five times. It would be the equivalent of the name Mike or John today. We don't know if this Alexander is the same Alexander mentioned several other times in scripture, but we do know that this Alexander is *not* the one mentioned in 1 Timothy 1:20. We also know that he is not the same man mentioned in Acts 19:33. Why? Because those two Alexanders lived in Ephesus. This Alexander is a coppersmith who lives in Rome.

Commentator William Barclay writes, "We don't know what had happened, but we can deduce that he caused Paul harm. It may be that Alexander was a renegade Christian who went to the magistrates with false and slanderous information against Paul. Maybe Alexander turned against Paul and sought to ruin him in the most dishonorable way."[35]

We don't know exactly what Alexander did, but we do know what he will get. In paraphrase, Paul says, "Don't worry about him, because God will repay him for the evil he has done. In due time, he will get what he deserves." Paul knows the Old Testament well. Psalm 62:12 says, "For you [God] will render to a man according to his work." And Revelation 2:23 says, "And all the churches will know that I am he who searches mind and heart, and I will give to each of you according to your works."

Friends, one day the books will be opened before the Lord Jesus Christ, and God will judge us based on our deeds. In God's accounting system, He doesn't miss a thing. His pencil is always sharpened; His hard drive never crashes. Every deed, every action, every motive, every thought that you and I have ever had—God has kept a record of that. Now, here is the encouraging news for us: believers will undergo a different type of judgment than unbelievers will. But we do know that every person will be judged.

An unbeliever is any person who has not trusted Jesus Christ as the sacrifice for his or her sins. When we stand before the Lord, we will either be able to claim that we have followed Christ and that His blood has covered our sins, or we will have to admit that we do not have a relationship with Jesus. For those who have never trusted in the Lord, Jesus will stand before God at the Great White Throne Judgment and deliver the verdict: guilty as charged. The sentence from the Great White Throne of Judgment is hell.

Thankfully, believers in the Lord Jesus Christ who have trusted in Him as their advocate and the Savior of their souls will be welcomed into heaven. Those who have been filled with the Holy Spirit, who have been born again in Christ—we will stand before what is called the *Bema Seat*. The Bema Seat is a word drawn from the Greek athletic scene. The Bema Seat is where the judge sat. After a race, the runners would walk up to the judge, and the judge would award them based on their performance in the games.

At the Bema Seat, we will be judged by our works. This judgment will not determine whether we go to heaven or hell; rather, it will determine what our rewards will be in heaven. Did you know that, as believers, we will be rewarded with dominion and authority in heaven given by the Lord Jesus Christ? But the key is this: we will all be judged. That's why Paul tells Timothy in essence, "Listen, don't worry about repaying evil for evil; God's going to do that." If someone is causing you harm, you don't have to repay evil for evil. Why? Because God is the avenger. Aren't you glad of that? God sees it all.

A Focused Servant Enduring to the End

Fifth, in verse 13, Paul offers the example of *a focused servant enduring to the end*. Paul calls for his cloak, the books, and above all else, the parchments which were at Troas. This is important because we learn something here about Paul's character. The cloak was a wool blanket-type outer garment. Paul needed it to keep warm in that cold, damp dungeon. The winter season was approaching. Then Paul says that he needs his books. The books were probably papyrus rolls. Then he says, "Bring the parchments," which were skins of animals, probably sheep or goats.

Why does he ask for all of these items? Paul is saying, "Even now, at the end of my life, I still want to study the Word." Isn't that amazing? Was Paul deliberately interested in writing a record of Christ's life? Wouldn't this be consistent with his emphasis in the pastoral Epistles for Timothy to "guard the good deposit of the gospel"? In essence, he is saying, "Timothy, Mark, bring me my books and bring me my parchments, because I want to show you what it means to guard the gospel."

Now, keep in mind that Paul did not simply decide, "Oh, I'm in a terrible situation, so now it's time for me to break out the Bible to try to get out of this mess." He wants to study at the end of his life because he started a disciplined life of study years ago, memorizing and meditating and reading and listening and praying to God. Now, close to the end, he's saying, "That's all I want to do. The Word is encouraging to me. I need and want to read the Word." Could you say, near the end of your life, that if you had to choose one item to keep with you, you would say, "Bring me my Bible"?

How has Paul been able to endure? He's moments away from death. How could he endure such suffering and isolation when all his friends had left him? He's all by himself in a Roman prison. He's already been tried before the Roman Proconsul. People probably traveled from far and wide to watch this man's trial because he had had the gall to challenge the Jewish leaders as well as the Roman government. In fact, Paul may have stood before Nero himself. Yet, just moments away from his death, Paul chooses to write an encouraging word that will speak to believers for eternity, and here it is. He says, one Person remained; "the Lord Jesus stood by me and strengthened me" (verse 17).

A Faithful Savior Strengthening His Followers

Let's focus now on Jesus, the sixth type of person Paul mentions in this book. Paul rejoices in *a faithful Savior strengthening His followers*. Instead of being depressed, Paul says, "The Lord stood by me and strengthened me so that through me the message might be fully proclaimed and all the Gentiles might hear it." A great scripture for you to memorize in a time of trouble is Psalm 139:8–10 (NIV): "If I go up to the heavens, you are there; if I make my bed in the depths, you are there. If I rise on the wings of the dawn, if I settle on the far side of the sea, even there your hand will guide me, your right hand will hold me fast." I'd be willing to guarantee that Paul knew this scripture.

At the end of Paul's life, he had gained so much encouragement from the Word that he was literally speaking and quoting and living and saturating his life with the Word of God. Friends, keep in mind that if you have not taken the time to memorize the Word *before* trouble comes, then you will not be able to repeat it and cling to it for help when you need it.

If you don't get excited about the Word of God, I believe that one of two things must be going on in your life. First of all, you may not be a believer, because believers have a strong desire for the Word. Second, you may be a believer, but you may be so saturated with sin and selfishness and pride and immoral behavior that you have been sidetracked from God. You no longer have a desire or a passion to hear and study the Word of God. You've strayed from your first love.

Ask yourself if you can put yourself into Paul's shoes and honestly say, "I love the Word so much that I am reading and sharing and speaking the Word to everyone I meet. God's truth is oozing out from every pore."

Now, you may be wondering, why do we bother to study the lives of men like Demas, Crescens, Luke, Mark, and Alexander? As we examine their lives, we see some faithful Christians who made it to the end and finished well. We also see some people who were sidetracked in their faith and did not finish well.

I want to ask you this question: what will you be remembered for? As the pages of your life turn, what kinds of entries are being written on them? Are they entries that you will be proud of later, or will you be ashamed?

I'm reminded of a friend who will always be remembered as a man who loved the Bible and loved Jesus with all of his heart. I'm talking about Dr. Spiros Zodhiates. Many of you know him well. Some of you have only heard of him. He was born to Greek parents on the island of Cyprus. He went to Cairo, Egypt, to study at the American University of Cairo. He then went to New York State University and received his doctorate in theology at Luther Rice Seminary. In 1946, he was invited to come to America to assist with the American Mission to the Greeks, which later became AMG.

When Dr. Zodhiates started his ministry in 1946, AMG had just two part-time workers in a one-room building. In 1966, they asked him to be president. Later, the organization's name was changed to AMG International. Today, this ministry reaches out to people in more than fifty-five countries around the world.

I had an incredible opportunity to meet Dr. Zodhiates toward the end of his life. Would you believe that he was still quoting scripture and talking about the Greek language? He kept telling us about Jesus and about all the things that the Lord had done in his life. Even in his final days, he was still guarding the gospel by sharing it with others.

On October 10, 2009, Dr. Zodhiates walked through time and eternity and finally got to meet his beloved Jesus face to face. At his funeral, people came from all over the world to speak on behalf of this great man and to talk about how much he had meant to them. One after another, they talked about his love for Jesus. Paul Jenks, the current president of

AMG, got up to speak. As he talked about Spiros, he kept returning to the subject of this man's deep, compelling love for Jesus.

When Paul Jenks ended his eulogy, a lady in the audience walked up to him and said, "Brother Paul, I noticed that at the funeral service, you didn't talk much about Dr. Zodhiates. You talked a lot about Jesus."

He replied, "Dr. Zodhiates would have wanted it that way."

Friends, I wonder what will be said at the end of your life. Will your loved ones be able to say, "He was so in love with the Lord Jesus Christ. That's all he talked about"? Will they be able to say, "Jesus was all she lived for. She really sought to be like the Lord Jesus Christ"?

When the end of your life approaches, will you be able to truthfully echo these words of the apostle Paul: "I have fought the good fight. I have finished the race. I have kept the faith. Henceforth there is laid up for me the crown of righteousness, which the Lord, the righteous judge, will award to me on that Day, and not only to me but also to all who have loved his appearing"? Will you be able to say that?

Endnotes

1. J. W. McGarvey, *J. W. McGarvey's Original Commentary on Acts* (Lexington, KY: Transylvania Printing and Publishing, 1872), http://www.searchgodsword.org/com/oca/view.cgi?book=ps&chapter=028&verse=001.

2. John McCray, as quoted by Elesha Coffman, "Christian History Corner: Captive Christians," from *Christian History* 46 (May 2002), http://www.christianitytoday.com/ct/2002/mayweb-only/52.0.html.

3. Hudson Taylor, as quoted at *Wholesome Words*: Worldwide Missions Notes and Quotes: "Missionary Quotes" compiled by Stephen Ross," http://www.wholesomewords.org/missions/msquotes.html.

4. R. Kent Hughes and Bryan Chapell, *1 and 2 Timothy and Titus: To Guard the Deposit* (Wheaton, IL: Crossway Books, 2000), 178.

5. Ibid., 189.

6. Bill Hull, *The Complete Book of Discipleship: On Being and Making Followers of Christ* (Colorado Springs, CO: NavPress, 2006), 24.

7. Billy Graham, *The Holy Spirit* (Waco, TX: Word, 1978), 147.

8. Ibid., 147.

9. John Wesley, quoted in "The Haystacks Effect," *Prayer Magazine*, http://www.prayermagazine.net/index.php?option=com_content&view=article&id=231:the-haystacks-effect&catid=49:features&Itemid=43.

10. Leroy Eims, *The Lost Art of Discipleship* (Grand Rapids, MI: Zondervan, 1978), 28.

11. Staff reporter, "Soldier's Pledge," *Baptist Press* (September 4, 2002) http://www.bpnews.net/printerfriendly.asp?ID=14164

12. John Stott, *The Message of 2 Timothy* (Downer's Grove, IL: IVP, 1973), 62.

13. "Suffering and Reigning with Jesus" (Sermon #547), Charles H. Spurgeon, *Spurgeon's Sermons: Volume 10*, electronic ed., Logos Library System (Albany, OR: Ages Software, 1998).

14. J. N. D. Kelly, *A Commentary on the Pastoral Epistles 1 Timothy 2 Timothy Titus* (New York: Harper & Row, Publishers), 182.

15. Hughes and Chapell, *1 and 2 Timothy and Titus*, 418.

16. Spiros Zodhiates, *The Complete Word Study Dictionary: New Testament*, electronic ed. (Chattanooga, TN: AMG Publishers, 2000), S. G2757.

17. John MacArthur, *2 Timothy* (Chicago, IL: Moody Press, 1996), 76.

18. Joe Lantz, *My Yacad: Who Am I? What Am I? and Why?* (Bloomington, IN: Author House, 2007), 13.

19. Story about Leonardo da Vinci, as told by John MacArthur in his sermon "The Reality of Sin: Man's Biggest Problem," *Bible Bulletin Board*, http://www.biblebb.com/files/mac/sg2217.htm.

20. Carl Ferdinand Howard Henry, *Twilight of a Great Civilization: The Drift toward Neo-Paganism* (Westchester, IL: Crossway, 1988), 23.

21. Stott, *The Message of 2 Timothy*, 83.

22. Ibid., 89.

23. Hughes and Chapell, *1 and 2 Timothy and Titus*, 225.

24. MacArthur, *2 Timothy*, 118.

25. "Baptist Faith and Message" from the website of the Southern Baptist Convention at http://www.sbc.net/bfm/bfm2000.asp.

26. Haddon Robinson, *Biblical Preaching: The Development and Delivery of Expository Messages* (Grand Rapids, MI: Baker Academic, 2001), 18.

27. Charles Haddon Spurgeon, "Sermons: Their Matter," *Spurgeon Fellowship Journal*, Fall 2008, http://www.thespurgeonfellowship.org/Fall08/hr_f08_1.htm.

28. Walter Kaiser, *Toward an Exegetical Theology* (Grand Rapids, MI: Baker Book House, 1981), 7–8.

29. George Whitefield, as quoted at *BrainyQuote*, "George Whitefield Quotes," http://www.brainyquote.com/quotes/authors/g/george_whitefield.html.

30. William Hendricksen, *Exposition of Thessalonians, Timothy, and Titus* (Grand Rapids, MI: Baker Book House, 1957), 315.

31. Winston Churchill, as quoted at *BrainyQuote*, "Winston Churchill Quotes," http://www.brainyquote.com/quotes/quotes/w/winstonchu124653.html.

32. "I'd Rather Have Jesus" lyrics by Rhea F. Miller; music by George Beverly Shea. Lyrics in the Public Domain.

33. William Barclay, *The Letters to Timothy, Titus, and Philemon* (Louisville, KY: Westminster John Knox Press, 2003), 213.

34. Hughes and Chapell, *1 and 2 Timothy and Titus*, 262.

35. Barclay, *The Letters to Timothy, Titus, and Philemon*, 246.